The Country Book of the Year

Dennis L. Furnell

David & Charles
Newton Abbot London North Pomfret (Vt)

British Library Cataloguing in Publication Data

Furnell, Dennis L
   The country book of the year.
   1. Country life – England – North Devon (District)
   I. Title
   942.3'52'08570924   S522.G7

   ISBN 0 7153 7878 3

Typeset by Northampton Phototypesetters Ltd
and printed in Great Britain
by Redwood Burn Limited Trowbridge and Esher
for David & Charles (Publishers) Limited
Brunel House Newton Abbot Devon

Published in the United States of America
by David & Charles Inc
North Pomfret Vermont 05053 USA

CONTENTS

For Ann and Robin

INTRODUCTION

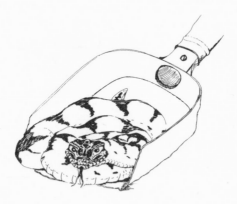

This book has its beginning with the season I find most fascinating, the autumn, with its golden light and the patterns made by falling leaves upon the gossamer-covered grass. I make no apology for this self-indulgence.

I am almost wholly absorbed in the English countryside, but my interest is not purely scientific. I still marvel, childlike, at the infinite variations of nature and the fascination is now much as it was when I was a child, when the foundations of my absorption were firmly implanted while roaming in the rolling hills and wooded valleys around a North Devon village.

There was a time when to open any matchbox in our household was a trial for my mother: she was never sure if the box would contain matches or a selection of grasshoppers or caterpillars or perhaps even a treasured lizard. Her long-suffering acceptance was stretched to the limit when I collected and brought home an adder. This venomous reptile put up with my ignorant handling without retaliation and even accepted temporary incarceration in a shoe box without a hiss of protest. Unfortunately, I was called to 'tea', or was it to wash my hands? – I know I considered the interruption unnecessary and during my enforced absence the adder decided it should resume its travels.

It removed itself from the confines of the utility brogues box and wandered, as snakes will, until it reached the sunlit front doorstep whereupon it decided that this was as good a place as any to have a nap and coiled itself up like a yellow and black table mat. How long it had been there before my mother discovered it is unknown, but it must have been deeply asleep or else had grown used to being handled by clumsy humans, for it allowed itself to be picked up on the coal shovel and deposited on the compost heap.

This episode might well have passed without comment had our elderly next-door neighbour not seen the creature slide from the compost heap into the safety of the long grass nearby. 'Arrr,' he said in his rich Devon accent, 'That be a viper, maid. They'm deadly!' Then without elaboration went back to weeding his vegetable plot. White with shock Mother staggered back into the house where I was rooting around trying to find my lost reptile. My innocent enquiry as to its whereabouts was met with an uncharacteristic outburst of rage, for my mother had realised that she had been playing unwitting host to a lethal creature. From that moment on I had strict instructions about bringing creatures into the house, reinforced by threats from my father on the dire consequences if I disobeyed.

Father's knowledge of the countryside was limited to the fact that it began outside our front door and continued as far as the eye could see. As a very urban Londoner he could appreciate a beautiful view, but could not comprehend my minute study of a patch of grass and its inhabitants. However, he did not discourage my activities, other than those which threatened the security of his home and family. In fact his lack of understanding made him, in some strange way, rather proud of the untypical child he had helped to produce and he would trot me out to air my limited knowledge to visiting friends who appeared in a never-ending stream, refugees from the bombing in London. A visitor would only have to say that they had been woken by the dawn chorus for my Father to produce me, like a small blond encyclopaedia, to identify the miscreants. This was a thankless task for me because having identified the birds responsible for the din, I could not answer the inevitable question of 'How can we stop the noise?'

This attitude, on the part of our visitors, lowered them in my childish eyes, for after listening wide-eyed to their stories of the London Blitz and marvelling at the fact that they could actually sleep in those interesting shelters with all that fascinating bombing going on, I found it odd that, when they arrived, grey-faced and weary, in our quiet home and fell exhausted into bed, the sound of a few birds would disturb them. After that their stories lacked credibility. I am now more understanding of their suffering, and my interest in the life to be found in a patch of grass or a bed of nettles is still as strong as it was then.

It is not really surprising that my childhood interest was in insects and grass and the denizens of the undergrowth, for these things are child-sized; children can relate to a jungle of grasses more easily than an adult can. For one thing they are closer to the ground.

I mourn the demise of the farm pond with its complex mosaic of life. The dragonflies hovered and darted over the duckweed, snapping up insects, their erratic flight on gauzy wings rustling as they passed close to me, making a sound like the crushing of a cellophane sweet-wrapper. As a child, the large dragonflies were beyond my abilities as a hunter of insects and I had to content myself with catching and examining the brilliant electric-blue damsel flies which flitted around the edge of a pond near my home. Those, and the frogs which plopped into the water at my approach, drew me like a magnet to this quarter-acre of stagnant water as a mariner is drawn to the wide Atlantic. If a sailor has salt water in his veins then I must have pond water and duckweed in mine. Put me next to a pond and I am a happy man.

The people of my childhood, those outside my family, also shaped

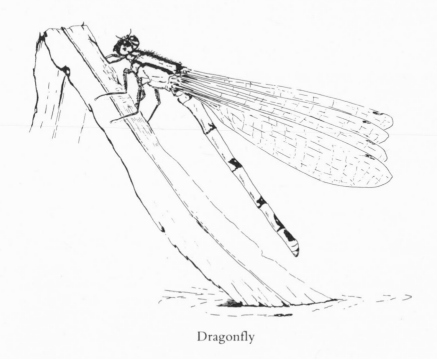

Dragonfly

9

my attitudes to the country. The farm workers who lived at one with the land and co-existed with the animals and plants were not as knowledgeable in scientific terms as their modern counterparts, but they were more dependent on their knowledge for their very existence. In the 1940s there were still families whose meals were directly supplemented by the produce of the hedgerow and rabbiting skills were still needed to provide vital protein. It was in the company of these people that my attitudes to the countryside and country pursuits were formed. Poaching was a way of life then, not a commercial enterprise as it is now. I was taught to catch trout from the local stream, by various methods, by the village bobby – blissfully unaware that we were poaching the local landowner's fish. But we took only enough for our own needs. No one considered this minor law-breaking in any way lessened the magisterial authority of the law, for the local publican would quake in his shoes if the bobby was seen during one of the frequent unofficial extensions of licensing hours which took place at his hostelry.

From an early age I was included in local hunting parties. They were not grand affairs, just a covert meeting of the local farm workers to test the rabbit population in the area with a motley collection of men, children, dogs and a sprinkling of ferrets. Everyone had a gun, but few had any ammunition; those that had made sure they saved the empty cartridge cases to be recrimped for the ammunition check at the next Home Guard meeting in the church hall.

This supply of cartridges, almost as much as patriotism, was the reason for the large numbers of volunteers for the Home Guard. My village, and I suspect many like it, would have presented an interesting fusillade of clicks, falling hammers on used cartridge cases, had the enemy actually invaded. But knowing the ingenuity of these hardy farm workers, they would have come up with something.

Knowledge of fieldcraft was gained under the tutelage of such people. How to approach a wild creature without disturbing it . . . how to recognise where a bird or animal is most likely to have its home . . . just how to use the skills with which nature endowed us in the first place, our eyes, our ears and our limited sense of smell. Even now, I tend to use binoculars only as a last resort when identifying a bird or animal in the field. These farming folk were at one with the seasons and the way the land responded at different times of the year, but most of their activities were channelled to come to fruition at one particular time, the harvest. This was the season when all the work, all the toil and all the unconscious planning yielded its reward: the grain for next year's bread, the seed corn for the following spring, the cider apples for next year's scrumpy and the Harvest Supper.

In the town, spring is the time of year when we look forward to a season of new beginnings, but in the countryside, now as in my childhood, the season of new beginnings is the golden-hearted autumn. Because of this and because it is my favourite time, this is where I shall start. . . .

(above) White-letter hairstreak; (below) pearl-bordered fritillary

1
OCTOBER

Like many writers before me I wish I had thought of the words penned by John Keats: 'Season of mists and mellow fruitfulness, close bosom friend of the maturing sun,' for they so exactly describe October, the crown prince of autumn. No other collection of words so aptly describes the feeling I get when watching the leaves changing colour and falling to the ground. Looking at the beautiful hues of red, gold and brown it is hard to imagine how the trees could bear to part with such finery, but part they must as the supply of lifegiving sap is withdrawn and the leaves drift down to provide nourishment for a whole world of tiny creatures below. Eventually the chemicals and nutrients released in the process of decomposition will be drawn up into the tree to repeat the process all over again. Quite a remarkable piece of recycling, carried out by an organism incapable of thought as we understand it.

In the hedge bottoms there is an air of bustle and excitement as the inhabitants prepare for the unknown trials of the coming winter. Fat insects help to make fat hedgehogs, and fat hedgehogs survive hibernation, to emerge in the spring thin but alive. So there is grim competition.

The insects have spent the warm days of summer growing in numbers and in strength and have hidden themselves where, hopefully, the hedgehog will not find them. But find them he must, or he will not rise from his winter sleep to start again the cycle of living and feeding and breeding. The insects that are n ot well enough adapted to fool the questing hedgehog succumb and swell old prickles's winter lining: only the successful insects remain.

It is nature's law that only the fittest shall survive; she is constantly searching for perfection and so the quadrille of natural selection dances on.

I am very fond of hedgehogs! In fact I use a picture of this 'urchin', as the old country folk used to call him, as my symbol and I take particular notice of his doings as he snuffles and sniffs along the hedge bottoms.

Hedgehog

Recently I had cause to marvel at the ability of these mobile scrubbing brushes to climb quite difficult obstacles. I was out in my back garden looking up at the night sky, trying to see the migrant birds I heard calling overhead as they passed by. My home, in a valley on the edge of the Chilterns in Hertfordshire, is on a main migration route and most nights in autumn and spring when the air is clear and the weather gentle, flocks of small birds fill the air with their contact calls as they wing down the valley between the chalk hills. On this particular night, although the conditions were perfect and the air was full of the calls of migrant thrushes, fieldfares and redwings, not one chose to cross the silver disc of the full moon. Suddenly from my right came the sound of heavy breathing accompanied by a sort of scraping, rustling noise as if a soul in torment was dragging itself along the path towards me.

Instantly my West Country background, with its tales of 'ghoulies and ghosties and long-leggety beasties and things that go bump in the

Hedgehog

night' leapt to the fore and the hair on the back of my neck prickled. I turned to look along the path and saw in the bright moonlight that it was quite unreasonably empty, whilst the scraping, rustling and heavy breathing grew nearer. Just when I was considering it prudent to go indoors, a movement on the top of the garden wall abolished all thoughts of flight. In the light of the moon the disconsolate figure of a hedgehog could be made out, wandering back and forth along the coping a clear 4 ft from the ground on my side and 6 ft from the ground on the far side.

Fetching a torch from the house, I was soon able to have a clear view of this Chris Bonington of hedgehogs as he wandered along the narrow coping, all the time emitting heartrending sighs. Quite suddenly, as if he was tired of being in the spotlight, he fixed me with a stare from his bright eyes, tucked his head, with its boot-button nose, between his front paws and rolled himself into a ball. Then he fell 6 ft to the slope on the far side. With a sound like rustling dry straw he rolled down the bank, coming to rest on the flat ground, where quite unaffected by his tumble he simply continued on his way.

I had previously heard that hedgehogs can fall a considerable distance without injuring themselves because their coat of spines acts as a shock absorber, so it was not the fall which amazed me. It was the fact that the hedgehog was on the wall in the first place, blithely walking along the top. The wall was smooth-sided and capped by an overhanging coping stone which projected some 3 in. At no point, it seemed, was there any place at which old prickles could have made the climb. But made it he had!

If there is no such a thing as a flying hedgehog, I shall have to enter him in the Guinness Book of Records as the first mountaineering urchin.

The migrants from the north and Scandinavia begin to arrive now on our eastern seaboard just as the last of the summer-breeding birds depart for the warmer climes of the Mediterranean and North Africa. The last swallows and martins are by now south of the Pyrenees, preparing to cross the sea at its narrowest point by Gibraltar.

Our ancestors used to think swallows and martins hibernated in the mud at the bottom of lakes and ponds, and we with our scientific knowledge think this attitude very strange. But the people who evolved this theory about swallow hibernation knew nothing of foreign travel, many of them had been no further than the nearest market town. Probably the furthest they would ever travel in their lives would be to a religious shrine in the nearest city, and this would have taken years of planning. So when they saw one day that the air above their pond was full of swallows and martins hawking for insects in the autumn air and that the next day not a single bird was to be seen, what was more logical than to presume they had all dived down to the muddy bottom to sleep? This belief was reinforced the following spring when one day, quite as suddenly as they had disappeared, they

Hobby with swift

were back again, and somnolent as if they had just been roused from a long slumber.

Nature abhors a vacuum, so when the summer visitors depart southwards new migrants come in from the north to replace them. Most of the birds going south are insect-eaters, like the swallows and flycatchers, and with them have gone the birds that prey on the insect-eaters.

On the chalk hills near my home one of the most spectacular sights is that of the hobby falcon dashing down the coombes of the chalk downland like a small jet fighter. This bird, now regrettably very rare because of habitat destruction and the effects of pesticides, is one of the most spectacular of the aerial acrobats. It is so fast and so manoeuvrable that it can catch a swift in flight. But it leaves in October, following the migrants to Africa.

The birds which take the place of the insect-eaters are seed and fruit eaters, like the fieldfare and redwing from the Scandinavian forests, birds which are hardy enough and adaptable enough to live through our milder winters and take advantage of the berries and seeds which our native birds cannot or will not handle. Over the centuries these Scandinavian migrants have helped to shape the distribution pattern of shrubs like the hawthorn and the sloe across our landscape. The seeds of these plants need to pass through the digestive tract of a bird before they will germinate, so the redwings gorging themselves on the bright red hawthorn berries will sow hawthorn seeds with their droppings. Scandinavian landscape gardeners with wings, shaping the hedgerows of England; Capability Brown was not the only creator of tree-lined vistas.

Fieldfares

Another tree which owes its spread to wild birds and animals is the crab apple. October is the time when these twisted and gnarled inhabitants of our countryside begin to drop their fruit, and the ground beneath the trees is invariably coated with a layer of apples. Because of their high acid content, crab apples keep well on the hedge bottom and provide food for small mammals like the woodmice, spruce little creatures with white waistcoats and shiny brown fur. These are the mice so beloved of Beatrix Potter for her children's stories, and I can never see a woodmouse without expecting it to drape its long tail over its paw and saunter off nonchalantly to some mouse soirée in a smart, Regency-style burrow.

Rooting around one October at the base of a particularly old

Woodmouse with apple

crab-apple tree in an equally ancient hedgerow, a movement attracted my attention and looking more intently I saw a woodmouse enthusiastically tucking into an apple. The fact that this normally shy creature was visible at all in the daytime was unusual enough, but to find one as tame as this was remarkable.

It appeared to take no real notice of me and allowed me to approach very close. At first I thought it was ill or injured, but at last discretion got the better of it and it scuttled off, I thought a trifle unsteadily. Puzzled, I examined the apple it had been eating and saw that it must have dropped from the tree some time before as it was brown and pulpy. The smell from it was reminiscent of the cider I was making at home and the reason for the mouse's 'devil may care' attitude became apparent. The apple was fermenting and probably my little mouse had a dose of Dutch courage and was under the influence of hedgerow cider.

I have seen butterflies under the influence after feeding on rotting plums, and a friend of mine who is a natural history artist has done some superb paintings of red admirals feasting on plums and commented on how intently they will suck the fermenting juice, ignoring close human inspection. But a boozy mouse was a first for me.

The hedgerow creatures grow ever busier as the end of the month approaches and the first frost of autumn touches the gossamer spiders' webs, making them shine like strings of seed pearls. The activity of finding and storing enough food for the coming winter becomes frantic as the shortening days and the gradual lowering of the

Spiders in grass

temperature prompt the hibernating animals to complete the process of fattening-up ready for the long winter sleep.

Not many animals go into deep hibernation in this country; most become dozy and just snooze during the coldest months, appearing occasionally when a bright spell occurs to have a look around and see if there is any food about. The few who really hibernate do so in a big way. The classic hibernator, the now not-so-common 'common dormouse', goes into a state which is hardly more than one stage above death, in that its body temperature drops nearly to that of its surroundings and its breathing becomes so slow as to be almost imperceptible. If one is handled in this state it can be, if you are so unkind, rolled across a table-top without waking up.

Dormice, with their golden fur and bright blackcurrant eyes, were a feature of my childhood, for they were quite common in the rich hedgerows of the North Devon countryside and I often used to have one as a pet. Unlike other rodents they do not seem to want to bite as a means of defence.

Alas they are now very rare and although there is a small colony living close to my cottage only the evidence of their presence under the hazel bushes can be seen: they make neat round holes in the fallen hazel nuts to get at the kernel inside. There are one or two disused nests in the hedgerows, made from shredded strips of honeysuckle bark; both of these plants are essential to dormice. The hazel provides food and the honeysuckle provides bedding and nesting material.

The decline in numbers of these inoffensive mice can be blamed entirely on modern agricultural methods and our pursuit of cheap food. Dormice need hedgerows to live in and to hibernate in, and the current vogue for hedgeless fields has spelt their end in many areas where once they were common.

Not only does the destruction of hedges remove the animal's habitat; it also restricts its ability to move about, for without adequate cover it cannot spread along the old highways which the hedges provided. Consequently dormice remain in isolated pockets of woodland and rough corners. Any that do venture out are quickly snapped up by owls and other predators.

Unfortunately hedge grubbing usually takes place in winter, when

Dormouse

farmers have fewer jobs to do with their expensive tractors. And so the dormouse is caught deeply asleep and unable to escape. Did those men at the Ministry of Agriculture who devised the grant for hedgerow removal ever consider the effect it would have on the wildlife of this country? I doubt it. We tend to blame the farmer for the tree and hedgerow destruction which has spread over our countryside in the last ten years, but all the time farmers are being exhorted by Government to produce more from the land at lower cost. When brought down to basics, to a farmer the land is first and foremost his factory. It has to make enough money to pay the bills and the tax man. Perhaps the only way that agriculture and wildlife will be able to live side by side is to provide cash incentives to the conservation-minded farmer to make it worth his while to keep some rough corners and preserve hedges. In other words, make conservation a crop!

The second and third weeks of October are often lit with a golden glow which means autumn, when the sun rises with still a trace of summer strength.

With the last of the summer sun comes the end of the year's butterflies. Brimstones flutter their leaf-shaped wings before beginning the long winter sleep in the depths of an ivy-clad tree, where they merge perfectly with the yellowing leaves. But before winter comes they have a last fling and flit about in the golden sunlight along the woodland rides at the back of my cottage.

Brimstone on ivy

Occasionally they are joined in their aerial manoeuvres by small tortoiseshells. These insects will overwinter, and often they are found indoors in dark corners sitting motionless and looking as if they were dead. Unfortunately the warmth of winter fires wakes them up and they flutter about using their stored energy before the spring. I usually take them down from their hiding places and put them in the outhouse where they will have a better chance. Another autumn butterfly is the comma, so called because the underwing has a comma-shaped mark stamped in white against the dark brown taffeta-like texture.

I have planted sedum and michaelmas daisies in my garden to provide nectar for the latecomers, and have my reward every time one of them visits the rather tangled flower beds. I am not all that keen on formal gardens.

October is also the 'conference season' for naturalists. This is the time of year when they are back from their summer observations, getting their winter plumage out of mothballs ready for a busy season of windy estuaries and cold woods. Now the light anoraks are sent to the cleaners and the polo-necked Aran jumpers are inspected, wellingtons checked for leaks and glove fingers counted. But there is time to gather in flocks at learned societies to try and outdo the other fellow's observation with a better one of your own.

For me, the highlight of the natural history scene is the annual gathering of the Entomological Society, both professional and amateur. Apart from my own lifelong interest in British butterflies and moths, I find this collective grouping of those who study insects and kindred 'bugs' fascinating largely because insects are, next to plants, the most important source of food for our wild creatures, and if it has been a good year for insects then it will have been a good year for all those species who depend on them. It also gives a guide as to what will happen in the year to come. Therefore, it's to the annual gathering I make my way to take the pulse of the countryside, so to speak.

Entomologists range in interests from those who spend their lives studying the fleas and parasites which inhabit the nest of the swift, to those who specialise in the large and hairy spiders which (irrationally) terrify me. In between are the people who study variations in the patterning on butterfly wings. At first this study appears to have little to do with anything, resembling the pursuit of prized variations by postage-stamp collectors. But the study of alterations in wing markings reveals curious facts which can be related to the species as a whole and can accurately forecast the decline or increase in a population of insects in a certain area.

The process of study goes something like this. A certain type of butterfly might normally have brown wings with five spots on the underside. In another area, quite close by, the same insect might have six spots on the wing. Study of both populations will show if the butterflies with six spots have any advantage over their five-spotted brothers. If they have, then they will multiply until six spots are the norm, in the two sites. However, if five spots are more successful the reverse will occur and the six-spotted version would be considered an aberration occurring only rarely, or when conditions were favourable enough to allow such mutants to survive.

Really this is a study of natural selection in miniature, and because insects tend to have short lives, one generation succeeds another quite quickly, the results of a study into genetics and inherited character-istics which uses insects in the wild, not in a laboratory, give a fairly good indication of man's effect on his environment.

Moths, for instance, have shown remarkable adaptation to human interference. The peppered moth is able to adapt its normal light coloration to a dark form in order to blend into the bark of soot-blackened trees in polluted city streets. But in more recent times, as soot pollution has decreased and the trees are becoming cleaner, the moths are duly becoming lighter again.

A hundred years ago entomology was the province of the country clergy, who did much of the more detailed work and identified many of the species for the first time. At the last annual conference I attended I saw only a few country ecclesiastics among the conventionally clad figures, so maybe they like many entomological species are in decline.

At these conferences there is usually much studying of specimens by gentlemen with small magnifying glasses in their hands and there was

Peppered moth; (left) black form of male. (right) normal male

one real professional with an arrangement of large magnifying spectacles strapped to his head. Needless to say he was studying minute wasps. Thank heaven for individualists in any walk of life. They make a grey world brighter.

There is great controversy at the moment as to whether individuals should breed native species of butterflies and release them in areas offering suitable foodplants, artificially raising the level of the population. We live in an almost entirely artificial environment already, and with the present pressure on native insects, my feeling is that they need all the help they can get. I for one will continue to release peacock butterflies in my garden and delight in seeing them at the end of the year feeding on the nectar from my michaelmas daisies.

Another autumn pursuit is game shooting. Some people dislike field sports and I both understand and sympathise with their point of view. My own attitude is coloured by the fact that in the area where I grew up, shooting was a way of life and it does have a valuable role to play in the conservation of habitat, which is crucial to wildlife.

Pheasants are not really wild creatures any more. They are part of the produce of farmland, a crop in the same way as corn or cabbages. To produce a good crop of corn the land has to be prepared in a certain way, and to produce a good crop of pheasants or partridges the land has to be managed in a certain way. It so happens that the requirement for game birds is just the same as that for the song birds and small mammals. Because pheasant chicks need insects for food no one ever sprays insecticide in or near pheasant coverts, so a well-run estate or farm where game is a crop has a larger population of wildlife to the acre than one which is intensively farmed. I do not make this point because I shoot pheasants regularly. I don't. It is just that until we find a better way of providing habitat for our precious wildlife, shooting should be looked at in its true perspective, as should all field sports.

I was recently given an assignment to cover a pheasant shoot at an estate near my home, for a national sporting magazine. The estate is in the guardianship, and the word is used advisedly, of one of Hertfordshire's oldest families. They have inhabited their estate since 1450 and are regarded by their tenants and workers with genuine affection.

Because of the current fiscal system the estate is now a company, with father and son in control, the major partner being the son. It is a successful highly mechanised farming enterprise and besides this it is stocked with pheasants and a few partridges. The shooting is organised on a double syndicate basis, with two separate groups of guns shooting on alternate weeks during the season.

25

Hen pheasant

The produce of these shoots is sold on the open market, as the produce of any other farm crop would be, but here the pheasants are living in an environment which is managed in the most natural way possible. The policy of the shoot is to keep minimum control over predators, this being exercised by the head keeper, a huge man with a voice to match, a voice calculated to make a poacher in the next county quake. On this estate the pheasants are not the 'tame chicken' variety, but strong-winged, wily birds used to fending for themselves in a natural environment.

The day of the shoot dawned brightly, amber light suffusing a clear sky, but with the promise of rain later, and, to make things more interesting for the guns a force-eight gale, which made the gnarled oaks in the parkland shudder and release the last tatters of their leaves in flurries.

After the draw for stands had taken place in the car park adjoining the keeper's cottage, the guns moved off to the first drive at the head of a field of kale: always a good place for pheasants, for they find food and shelter in the avenues of stems which form a pheasant-sized forest. The beaters advanced under the stentorian instructions of the keeper, who had to use the full majesty of his vocal powers to keep in touch over the rising wind.

The first birds broke cover, and using the wind they went up into the air like vertical-take-off aircraft, giving no one a chance of a shot. I was fully occupied with my camera, but had I been shooting the pheasant population of Hertfordshire would have been in no great danger. As the drive progressed a number of these feathered rockets fell to the guns and towards the end there was a shout of 'partridge' as a winged projectile whipped over the hedge, to fall to a gun on my left and be collected by a cheerful labrador.

The drive through the wind-lashed kale ended, and guns and beaters moved on to an area of mature oak and beech woodland surrounded by a stand of three-quarters-grown larches, beautiful trees glowing in bonfire colours. This second drive had a different flavour, as did the wildlife disturbed by the beaters as they moved through the reddening underbrush. A fox, resplendent in his autumn coat, dashed from the wood and ran down a broad ride leading to the family house – a house, incidentally, built on the site of a fourteenth-century monastery. No one raised a gun to him and a sleepy owl which flew from the wood received similar immunity. By midday the threatening clouds broke, but in place of the expected rain, came hail of battering intensity which drove us all, guns, beaters and dogs, to seek shelter and an early lunch.

One of the dogs, a spaniel called Nell, had caught my attention during the day. Apart from having the panting enthusiasm which characterises this breed, and a certain air of enjoyment, she had been trained by the father of her present master to retrieve shot birds in a singular way. Her original owner had continued to take an active part in shooting until an advanced age. The only real havoc the years had wreaked on him was a stiffening of the back which meant he could no longer reach down to take the bird from the dog. So Nell was trained to deliver the game sitting up on her back legs. Some dogs have real personality and Nell had a superabundance.

One of the criticisms levelled at all field sports is that the people who take part in them are unthinking snobs. In my experience of field sports I have found fewer snobs engaged in this particular pastime than in many others, and those exhibiting any supposed superiority over beaters or workers will soon find their ego punctured. To a degree it is true that shooting is a sport for the relatively well off, for even a modest foreign gun costs as much as a colour television set; and because it is an all-winds-and-weathers sport, many people do not find it to their liking.

The objection that field sports impose cruelty on wild creatures is, in essence, quite justified. However, the fact of the matter is, there is a market for game birds, and they do not lend themselves to intensive rearing or factory farming. If people wish to partake of roast pheasant – and they do – we have a choice: either we have pheasants reared and

27

Nell with her owner, Godfrey Kent, showing her unusual method of retrieving

shot in their natural environment, or we have rows of deep-litter rearing sheds, where birds for the table live in a controlled environment, beaks permanently clipped to stop feather-pecking, fed with high-protein food with added antibiotics to prevent disease, and at the end of their sunless existence despatched on the back of a lorry to a factory, where people are paid to kill them.

The clocks go back at the end of the month and the long evenings begin to make themselves felt. The first of the winter gnats dance on the still evening mist and late moths whizz into lighted windows, diverted from their search for food or a mate.

Other denizens of the evening are also making the most of the available food before they hang themselves up for the winter hibernation. These are bats, creatures which are steeped in legend and folklore and have been attributed, quite incorrectly, with the desire to spend a large part of their waking hours frantically trying to entangle themselves in young maidens' hair.

How this particular old wives' tale ever gained credence is a mystery. Bats hunt their prey on the wing by an incredible system of echo location, outstanding in its effectiveness. A stream of high-pitched squeaks is produced by the animal and these squeaks, most of which are beyond the limits that human ears can detect, bounce back from the bat's surroundings and are picked up by their acute sense of hearing.

Noctule bat

29

Using this system the bat can home in on a gnat and catch it without ever seeing the creature, and do so in pitch darkness among the twigs of a tree. The bat never collides with anything, so how it could fail to see a great big human is beyond me.

Bats are in other ways, too, marvellous animals. Their long fingers have become adapted, over a million years, to form the framework for one of the most efficient wings in nature. Unlike a bird, which uses the whole of its forearm as the basis for the wing, the bat, in effect, flies by flapping its hands at the wrist. The thinly stretched skin between the fingers forms a flying surface, a means of propulsion and a method of steering all in one neat package.

In Britain there are fourteen species of bat although some of these, like the mouse-eared bat, are thought to be visitors to this country. They range in size from the tiny pipistrelle, which weighs only $\frac{1}{4}$ oz with a wingspan of approximately $7\frac{3}{4}$ in to the large high-flying noctule bat. A female noctule can weigh as much as $1\frac{1}{2}$ oz and have a wingspan of 15 in.

All bats hunt during the hours of darkness. They are the night shift of the aerial world and come on duty when the birds go home to roost. They fill much the same niche in nature at night as swallows, swifts and martins occupy in daylight hours, but, unlike birds, bats generally do not migrate far from their roosts when the cooler weather comes; instead they congregate together in holes in trees, caves or the roof spaces of old houses and churches. The practice of wiring-up openings in church towers to stop bats from getting in may have helped the spread of death-watch beetle in church timbers, for without the bats to catch the beetle during its free-flying stage, when it emerges to start laying its eggs, there is no natural predator. In the past, the 'bats in the belfry' would have had death-watch beetle on their menu.

Although bats hibernate they do not sleep throughout the winter, and can often be seen on mild days. Even in quite cold weather they will move from one roost to another. They seem to be spread all over these islands, but are concentrated in areas where there is more woodland and water and therefore more insects, for bats in this country live entirely on insects.

As a child I had a favourite hollow yew tree which was a roosting place for pipistrelles and long-eared bats. This tree, which had an extremely large hole in it about 5 ft from the ground, stood in the local churchyard, it was probably planted before the Norman church was built. Reaching inside the cavity, I could catch hold of one or two bats and would bring them out into the light to marvel at their soft brown fur and their tissue-paper wings, then put them down at the edge of the hole and watch them scurry back into the safety and darkness of the tree, squeaking furiously as they jostled their companions hung up inside.

This was a source of constant interest and each week I would climb my 'bat tree', as I called it, to check that my charges were still in residence. I was never disappointed, but one day I had a shock which nearly made me fall out of the tree. I had put my arm inside the hollow as usual and had gently grasped a protesting long-eared bat, but as I withdrew my jumper-clad arm it caught on something inside the hole.

As usual when snagging a pullover on some projection I pushed my arm back until the snag came free; however, as I drew arm and bat out of the tree I found I had not caught one bat, but two, and the one caught on my sleeve was the mother and father of all bats, with a wingspan nearly a foot across and looking very annoyed. This was my first sight of a noctule bat and the nervewracking experience was completed when it opened its mouth to show a fine set of needle-sharp teeth and chattered in high-pitched annoyance at being hitched up on a piece of Fair Isle.

Moving slowly I put the long-eared bat back on the tree and it scrambled inside. Then I faced the task of disentangling its large relative. Gingerly I grasped the creature with my other hand and as it did not make any move to bite it was soon freed and could be examined in detail. It was quite unlike any bat I had ever seen before. Its eyes were large and its face was more like that of a small fox than a bat. The fur was golden brown and silky and the wings, which flapped as I handled it, were not delicate like those of the small bats I had handled in the past but thick-boned and leathery.

Using the talent for subterfuge inherent in all small boys, I smuggled my find back into my bedroom to examine it at leisure. I was not sure that my mother would share my enthusiasm for the 'largest bat in the world' as I had christened my new friend, especially after the incident with the 'adder'. Having placed it in a box I looked in a book for the identity of my gigantic find. Being quite sure it was new to science I was bitterly disappointed to find its true identity. 'Fairly common' the book said. If it were all that common why hadn't I seen one before? Such is the egotism of youth!

But the book did give valuable information as to the bat's diet: 'in captivity – will eat mealworms.' The only problem was it didn't say what a mealworm was. I could only presume it was similar to any other kind of worm so that is what I offered my guest, who now hung from the side of a margarine box like a small tightly rolled umbrella. Either he was a very polite guest or perhaps hunting had been poor; if he disliked earthworms he didn't show it and munched my offerings with gusto. A subsequent visit to the small flour mill at the bottom of the valley solved the mealworm identity problem and I came away with enough of these creatures in a tin to keep Dracula well fed, let alone one medium-sized bat, and a promise of as many as I could use for the future.

Much to my surprise the bat became tame and would come squeaking to the front of the cage at my approach. It would allow itself to be handled without protest, providing a mealworm was imminent, and I managed to keep my prize a secret from my family for some time despite the procession of children who seemed to come and go at bat-visiting time.

This happy state of affairs could have continued had he, the bat, not decided to change sex and produce an infant: a minuscule bundle which clung to its mother's fur. This was such stupendous news it could not be kept to oneself. The world must know. My admission at breakfast that my bat had had kittens was greeted with blank disinterest. Not really surprising when you consider that the night before the Luftwaffe had levelled a considerable part of Plymouth and my father had been involved in removing the survivors from the ruins. His red-eyed enquiry was couched in a 'how nice' tone of voice and it was clear that no one was in the mood to hear about the most momentous event in natural history since the *Origin of Species*.

Presuming parental approval I finished my breakfast and went upstairs to return moments later with the mother and child. What Hitler had failed to do, my bat achieved instantly; there was pandemonium in the household. Both my parents were convinced that the Curse of the Vampire had become a reality and I was the one who had brought it upon the family. As the large maternal and quite affectionate bat climbed up my arm, they thought it was heading straight for their child's jugular . . . . It was only with great difficulty that I managed to get the bat out of the house unscathed and back to the safety of the tree by the church.

I will draw a veil over the subsequent discussion; it was a case of logic being overruled by parental authority. Needless to say bats were put on the list of prohibited creatures, but that episode with the noctule left me with an abiding interest in and deep fondness for them.

2

NOVEMBER

The first frost of the year has usually been and gone by now and the gales which sweep the land in the first few weeks of the month have stripped the remaining leaves from the trees, leaving all but a few standing naked, their bare arms raised to the sky in supplication.

A few trees keep their covering until the end of the month, the ash and the noble oak, plants so native to these islands that without their presence England simply would not be England. The oak is the corner-stone of the wildlife of this country, for in its dense foliage live more forms of insect life than in any other native tree, and on this abundance of creepy-crawlies lives a host of higher animals and birds.

In fact the oak plays host to so many insects they almost strip off the summer growth of leaves. The tree then produces a second crop, sometimes called the Lammas growth, because it often happens after the first day of August or Lammas Day. These new leaves are flushed with red as if the tree were having a dress rehearsal for the coming autumn.

The English or pedunculate oak produces acorns rounded at the tip, but on its near relative, the sessile oak, they are more pointed. In some areas the two types interbreed and their offspring are indeterminate in shape.

The sessile oak, Latin name *Quercus petraea*, is said to produce straighter wood than the pedunculate oak, *Quercus robur*, although the shape of the tree is often considerably altered by man. The 'goblin oaks' of Dorset and parts of Devon have been shaped by the practice of coppicing or lopping the upper branches for firewood and charcoal, twisting and stunting their straight growth and making them look supernatural.

However, the main reason why our forefathers had such reverence for the oak was economic rather than supernatural. As a building material for ships or wood-framed houses it was unmatched. It provided fuel for the peasant's fire, charcoal for his forge and forage for his swine, for in the 'pannage' season, as the time for the fall of acorns is called in the New Forest, the swine were let loose to forage for them. Too bitter for humans to eat directly, but when converted into pig meat acorns are welcome enough.

Even when the pig was dead the oak still had a role to play, for it was the smoke from the tannin-rich wood which cured hams in the chimney throat. Most old country farmhouses and cottages have inglenook fireplaces with a beam as part of the structure, and examination will nearly always reveal a hook or bar from which meat was hung for smoking in the winter.

Examination of early furniture also reveals the dependence of our ancestors on the oak. Most of the chests which have survived from the time of good Queen Bess are made of oak and much of this timber was second-hand, having first served time as ship's timbers or the frame of a barn.

In the time of Elizabeth I, a squirrel could have jumped, had he felt so inclined, from the border country of Wales to the outskirts of London without having to come down to the ground, so dense were

Oak chest

34

the oak woods. But by the end of the 1650s iron-working and shipbuilding requirements had so eroded the forests that they had become split up into pockets of woodland with farmland and grazing between. The whole economic structure of the community changed. The strips of newly cleared open land became boundaries to estates and the first steps were taken to enclose the land. The peasant could no longer be independent of the local landowner and run his cattle and swine in the open forest for free food. He had to till the land to provide both food for his family and food for his stock. And so the loss of the forests led to the beginnings of urban life.

Oak wood is dense and hard, as anyone who has had to saw oak logs will know. The sapwood rots fairly quickly, but the heartwood, with its lovely silver grain, is rich in tannin and resists attack by fungus.

The method of seasoning was dictated by our forefathers' lack of power: when the tree was felled it was simply left on the forest floor for years, until the outer sapwood rotted, leaving only the heartwood. This had two benefits;.the outer wood was of little value and to remove it by sawing, which had to be done by hand, did not pay; also it lightened the weight of the tree when the time came to move it, often ten years or so later.

Where rivers and streams were available, they were probably used to transport trees over longer distances, a practice which may have led to the method of seasoning oak which was used in the Middle Ages. Some of the trees which were floated downstream would have stuck in mudbanks and been abandoned, to be found years later. When the recovered baulk was sawn or split it would be found to have hardened and cured to an undreamed-of durability, and so the practice of immersing oak and other hardwoods in ponds for seasoning, for periods of fifty to a hundred years, became widespread. The mud sealed the wood in an airtight, insect-proof shield under water until it was needed.

Many of our cathedrals are built of timbers prepared in this way, and where the original instructions to the craftsmen are still available references can often be found to the length of time the roof timbers were to be seasoned. The instructions must have been reliable for most of the buildings are still standing.

Most of the timber was riven – split with a wedge – rather than sawn. This practice, as well as being economical of effort, allowed the wood to break along its weakest point, taking the natural twisting and stress out of the finished plank, so when the beam was shaped by an adze it would not warp or twist.

Trestle saw

One of my earliest jobs in Devon as a child was collecting twigs to be made into faggots for fire-lighting, and when older and stronger I cut 'sticks'. These were not sticks in the accepted sense, but fallen branches 6 in on the round. They were slung across a trestle saw-horse and cut through with a saw which resembled a five-bar gate with a hand-forged blade as the bottom rung. No one could remember who had made the monster, but it was very old and very effective. Sawing 'sticks' was the ultimate punishment, dreaded by one and all. There is a saying that he who buys logs gets warm once, but he who cuts logs gets warm at least twice. I can vouch for the truth of that statement, having sweated and strained over the wood for our living-room fire – a monster with an incredible appetite for wood and a heat output which was to say the least marginal. Nevertheless I am a fan of log fires. There is something primeval about the dancing flames of a real fire; the dust and mess are a small price to pay for the pictures that can be conjured from the leaping flames.

So with the first frost comes the process of obtaining logs for the winter ahead, and the choice of wood is vital. In my area beech is the predominant forest tree: in Victorian times it was known as the 'Chiltern weed'. It burns bright and gives out a lot of heat, but does not last long. The good old oak burns long and hot and the embers will start a new fire easily; and neither of these woods spits sparks. The tragic elm whose wood lies in abundance, the aftermath of the devastating Dutch elm disease, is a timber not greatly thought of as firing by our forebears, but cut and left to dry for a year it is as good a firewood as you could wish for. Its unpopularity stems from the fact that it is difficult to cut and almost impossible to split, but its strength and resistance to cracking, because of the random fibre of the grain, made it ideal for wheel-hubs on farm carts.

The Queen of firewoods is the ash, straight-grained, easy to chop and saw, and wet or dry burning with a bright flame; it makes a good bed of embers, rather like holly which has similar characteristics. Of the softer woods, silver birch is the only one I consider usable, but it does burn away very quickly giving out little heat. The fruit woods, such as apple, pear and cherry, make excellent firewood and scent the room as they burn, but I rarely have the heart to burn them as they are marvellous for carving and making furniture. In consequence I have a collection of fruitwoods which will never be used if I live to be a hundred.

Walnut

Several years ago I was given a whole walnut tree, which had stood on the site of a convent. Most of the older walnut trees in this country seem to stand where religious orders once had their dwellings. This particular tree had fallen victim to a severe gale and because I was looking for some walnut to carve the owner generously gave it to me. With the help of some friends I cut the timber into manageable lengths and then into planks. The result was a mass of offcuts which even I could not think of a reason for keeping, so they were consigned to the woodpile. Putting some of these on to the fire one evening we noticed that the room was beginning to take on a sweet smell reminiscent of incense. I can only presume the long-departed nuns used the leaves and twigs as an offering in the absence of real incense.

One of the additional benefits of burning wood is that the ashes are good for the garden. Unlike ashes from coal or smokeless fuel they can go straight on the ground without being weathered as they do not contain noxious sulphur which would kill the plants.

Conifer woods should however be avoided like the plague – unless you don't mind having your house burned down around your ears. I use pine and other softwoods as kindling to start the fire off, but even then a really efficient spark guard is vital; all resinous woods sputter violently and a stray spark can shoot a considerable distance, setting fire to furnishings and fabrics.

Pine cone

As the last of the leaves fall the structure of the tree becomes apparent. The old story that the shape of a tree is the same as the shape of its leaf ribs is quite a reliable guide. For instance, if you hold a dead sycamore leaf up to the light, you will see the central spine of the leaf echoes the trunk of the parent tree and the ribs which radiate from it form a very creditable representation of a sycamore. Even the twigs are visible if you look closely.

When all the leaves are gone and the trees are left without their protective canopy, the squirrels can be seen more clearly running up and down the branches. At first they are nervous and the slightest disturbance will send them leaping for cover, but as the cooler weather approaches their inbuilt need to stock up the winter larder takes precedence over fear, and they scurry down the trunks in search of nuts and seeds.

Sadly the native red squirrel is confined to Scotland, Wales, the West Country and Norfolk, some say driven from its natural habitat by the imported grey squirrel. Having seen both grey and red squirrels living side by side, however, I tend to think it is man rather than the 'tree rat',

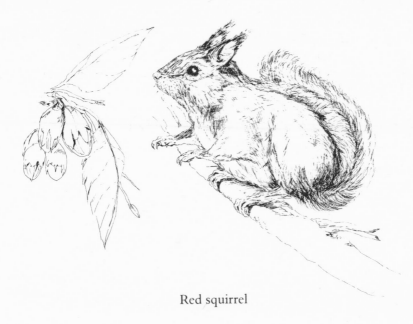

Red squirrel

as the grey is nicknamed, who has driven out this beautiful creature.

The red squirrel is a native of mature woodland and is far more a tree dweller than his North American cousin, who will spend much of his time on the ground and also travel long distances overland. The red tends to travel from tree to tree and along hedgerows, and destruction of hedgerows and woodlands and reafforestation with conifers has meant that populations of red squirrels have become isolated. Any killed by disease or predators are not replaced by outsiders and in time they just die out.

The gap in the ecosystem is filled by the more mobile greys and any red squirrel making his way to grey-squirrel territory will find a hostile reception. Even without the introduction of the grey squirrel the red would probably have declined in the face of modern agriculture. Like many other forms of wildlife it needs the shelter of the hedgerows.

An animal which is showing an opposite trend in population is the fallow deer. Intensive agriculture suits deer and the modern fashion for cereal crops in big fields means they have an abundance of food: also they like to feed at night on open ground so they can see their enemies coming. Modern farms need less people to the acre to work the land, so human disturbance is at a minimum. Just the right conditions for a large herbivore or grazing animal.

Autumn is the time of year when the deer mate or 'rut', when the antlered bucks gather a harem of does around them and defend their territory from invading males. Large open fields are perfect for the rut as the buck can keep an eye on his group of females and also spot any approaching males. In consequence of their successful breeding, fallow, or park deer, as they are sometimes known, have multiplied, despite considerable road casualties and poaching by morons with shotguns who wound more deer than they kill.

Fallow deer live in the wood adjoining my cottage and it is not uncommon to see one of these lovely creatures carrying the effects of a shotgun blast on its dappled side. I am not against the killing of deer, but I am violently opposed to wounding any creature, and to use a weapon which was designed for close-range work on smaller animals and birds is inhumane.

Blackbird

As autumn progresses the garlic mustard in the hedgerow turns straw brown and the elders droop under the weight of their umbrellas of purple fruit. Blackbirds and thrushes foraging in the undergrowth are joined at this time by the package tourists from Scandinavia, the fieldfares and redwings. These brash newcomers chortle and chuckle around the hawthorns, stuffing themselves on the bright red berries and gorging on the sloes which now stand out on the gaunt branches of the blackthorn hedge like ripe grapes on the vine.

It is a pity these small members of the plum family are so incredibly acid for they look deliciously appetising with their plump purple skins full to bursting with juice, suffused with a silk-like bloom. The thrushes and blackbirds seem to enjoy them, however, and as I sit and

40

look out of my window I can see the bustle of activity which heralds approaching winter.

The gradual fall of leaves shows the wood behind my cottage in all its naked beauty and the larches which compose the main body of the wood show through the ash trees which surround them. I am not enamoured of conifer woodland as a general rule, but the larch is an exception. Being deciduous it changes its appearance as the season progresses, now standing tall and proud in full autumn finery of flame and gold, a vivid coat of drying needles which soon will be shed leaving a delicate tracery of branches against the winter sky.

Apart from the fact that larches do not have the alien look which other conifers have in the English landscape, they are rich in wild creatures and birds who find safe nesting sites in the thick foliage. As the tree sheds its garment small nests can be seen in the branches; goldcrests have been at work all summer weaving tiny hammocks for their minute eggs, no larger than a garden pea. The goldcrests' nests, constructed from spiders' webs and pieces of grass and leaves, will withstand the downpours of the winter and will not fall until spring.

Sparrowhawk

Most of all, for me, the larches mean sparrowhawks, brigands in football jerseys who dash pell-mell along the side of the wood, twisting and turning this way and that, seeking some unsuspecting bird who has allowed greed to take the place of caution. A streak of blue-grey, a blaze of yellow eyes, and where a flock of feeding, chattering redwings were stuffing themselves on rose hips there is now only confusion and a cream feather drifting down to join the debris at the hedge bottom.

·Although they kill and eat the birds which come to my bird table – sometimes they even take chaffinches from the block of beech which stands outside the window – I admire all birds of prey, and have a distinct fondness for the dashing sparrowhawk. They suffered so badly from the effects of pesticides in the early 1960s, but they are slowly inching back into their old haunts – only to find that some of these havens of woodland and coppice have been replaced by huge open fields. They are not able to adapt as well as their mouse-hunting relation the kestrel, so sadly they will never be as numerous as they were in my boyhood days. Then, any walk would be punctuated by the speeding flight of the female hawk, almost twice the size of her blue-backed mate, twisting and turning in the close confines of a stunted oak wood which clung to the side of our steep coombe. To watch them circling over the edge of the wood in the evening, their broad rounded wings held stiffly as they completed their patrol, was a joy. It is easy to see how gamekeepers, during the early part of this century, were able to kill so many sparrowhawks, for even now I can tell, almost to the minute, when the hawks will spiral up from the wood in the evening, and depending on the wind direction I can even tell where they will spiral down for the roost again. The gamekeeper could wait in ambush, and another hawk would join the rotting carcasses on the gibbet. Keepers are now a more enlightened breed and do not always shoot birds of prey, allowing them the occasional pheasant chick.

All birds of prey are protected in this country, but in practice little can be done to stop the few misguided keepers that still exist. It is all too easy to condemn the gamekeeper because he pulls the trigger, but he is not the only killer. Some fault must lie at the feet of the employer whose main interest is to get as much shooting from the land as possible and to make sure the keeper produces pheasants like starlings in the sky. He doesn't question his keeper's methods as long as the birds are there when he wants to shoot.

This type of employer encourages the keeper to kill anything with a hooked beak or sharp teeth. Perhaps the employer as well as the keeper should be fined when protected species are killed; even better would be a plan to give some financial aid to conservation-minded shooting syndicates who would be prepared to allow a good head of natural predators on their land.

What of the other creatures the fall reveals in the leafless hedgerows? The fairies of the wood, the long-tailed tits, are gathering in small parties and zit-zitting along the side of the lanes. Not long ago I was

Long-tailed tit

sitting watching for a fox whose earth was nearby; the animal had a very light coat and did not seem to mind venturing out during the day. I had settled down for a long wait. To the left of where I sat on a small grassy bank was an old, gnarled hawthorn bush which still bore the tattered remnants of last year's red leaves on its branches. The afternoon was quiet and although there was a nip in the air the atmosphere had a soporific effect. My eyes were getting heavy and I was beginning to nod off when, from the hawthorn, there came a quiet sound like a whisper. I turned my head but could see nothing. The whisper became more insistent. As I have said, being a West Countryman by upbringing I am only marginally sceptical about the supernatural and I was beginning to wonder if an ancestor was trying to tell me something but had picked a bad line from the hereafter, when I saw the author of the whispering.

A flock of long-tailed tits were working their way through the hawthorn with characteristic thoroughness. They were hanging in all sorts of crazy poses exploring the rough bark with extreme care and all the time they searched they were uttering quiet whispers to one another, as if to say 'Here look at this, but don't tell the others.' 'Have you ever seen a caterpillar like this one? But keep it to yourself.' I have watched and drawn these delightful birds for years, but this was the first time I had ever heard this whisper and I have been extremely close to flocks many times before.

I sat quietly trying to look like an old log, and must have succeeded for the party came closer and closer to me. Then one bird gave the characteristic 'zit' call, flew straight from the hawthorn and landed on the tweed sleeve of my Norfolk jacket. The tweed was chosen from a swatch of Harris material because of its neutral hedgerow colouring, and obviously the camouflage was as good as I had hoped. The bird explored the surface of the sleeve with interest, even pulling up a thread of the material to see how many insects were hidden in the weave.

There are times when the natural world gives all the satisfaction a man could wish for and this was one of those times.

The minute bird, so light that I could not detect his weight on my arm, hopped around on my sleeve completely oblivious of the fact that I was inside. After a few seconds it decided that Harris tweed was not as rich in insect life as hawthorn, and giving its contact call to the flock it flew off. The rest of the flock followed, several birds repeating the example of their leader, briefly landing on my jacket before moving on. I became aware of an uncomfortable tight feeling in my chest and realised that I had been holding my breath whilst this visitation by fairies was in progress. My exhalation was such that the nearest bird, which was still only a few feet away, took fright and the flock moved off in mild panic. They soon settled down to feeding again about 20 ft away, and I could hear the contact call – but not the whisper; and although I have been very close to feeding flocks of these beautiful and dainty birds since, I have not heard it again. I can only be glad to think I was privileged to eavesdrop on a very private moment in their lives.

Where you find long-tailed tits you will usually find the smallest of British birds, the goldcrest – sometimes called the goldcrest wren. It is

Goldcrest

not a wren, but its minute size and perky manner as it moves in and out of the bushes has led to the misnomer. From a distance they look nondescript little birds, but close to you can see the plumage is olive green and above the bright eye there is a stripe of golden-yellow bordered with black. They are chubby little birds with beaks like black gramophone needles and an expression on their faces not unlike a Walt Disney bluebird.

After the cold winters of the early 1960s which killed 90 per cent of the resident population, they are now becoming more common and can be seen in gardens even in the centre of big towns. They do not normally come to a bird table, but on the odd occasion they have visited lard I had hung on a string for the blue tits, hovering just like humming-birds and pecking at the fat, defying the tits to come near. If one lands on the fat for a more relaxed meal he guards the food by fanning his tiny wings threateningly, and the blue tits, themselves pugnacious feeders, are frightened off, an amusingly David and Goliath match.

This is the time of the year when I re-erect the bird table. One of the first things I do in spring is take them down and put them in the barn. Apart from the sun splitting the wood and destroying the varnished surface, vital if you are to keep the table clean throughout the winter, the birds which are starting to nest nearby will have less chance of establishing a territory because they will be constantly on the offensive, driving off intruders who are only dropping in for a meal. Besides, the practice of feeding birds into the spring can result in the death of the early broods – when the parents try to feed them scraps from the table, their digestive systems cannot cope. So my bird tables go up in November and come down in the last week of March. There are a few disgruntled visitors to the spot for a week or so after the tables disappear, but they soon settle back into the pattern of finding natural food again.

Likewise it takes a week or two in autumn before the birds find the table; but find it they do. Siting it is important, more important than its design, for almost any flat surface on the top of a pole will do. But if you put it too close to a fence or a shed it is a certainty that the local cats will regard it as a device put there solely for their benefit, and the few birds you do get will not be able to feed under the baleful gaze of next door's pussycat.

If you are fortunate enough to live near a wood, then it is a good idea to place the table in line of sight of the wood. Your visitors will be more varied and because they know that home and safety are only a few wingbeats away they will feed with more confidence.

There is nothing nicer, in my view, than to sit indoors on a frosty day and watch the constantly changing scene on a bird table, especially when your visitors include such colourful creatures as jays and nuthatches. It is one of the few distractions which beats television for children. My own son will watch the table for hours on and off during the day.

If you are an accomplished carpenter then your bird tables can be made with automatic seed-hoppers or peanut-dispensers built into them, but if you just want somewhere for the birds to come for a feed, a metal tray nailed to a post 5 ft high will do perfectly well. Knock a hole into one corner of the tray and you can hang a wire nut-basket from it; there you have the almost perfect set-up. The only thing to remember is that the table should be kept clean and well stocked, for after a month or so the regular visitors will be expecting food and if none is available it is likely, in very cold weather, that they will starve to death, having become conditioned to expect nourishment from you.

3

DECEMBER

To describe December as winter can seem a little previous, for in this month of contrasts and feverish activity leading up to one of the most significant events in the Christian calendar, come days when the weather is mild as spring. Only the brevity of the daylight hours reminds us that winter is yet to come.

December also brings the start of a favourite winter field sport, pigeon shooting. To those who have an aversion to field sports it can be justified as being beneficial to farmers, for a wood pigeon eats large quantities of valuable food crops. The wood pigeon is generally believed to be one of the most difficult of all birds to kill with a shotgun, so much so that a mythology has grown up as to its ability to resist the pentration of shot. Some shooters, after missing behind, in front, or to both sides of a jinking 'quist', have stated that the birds can draw their feathers around their well-muscled bodies to present a bullet-proof waistcoat to the onrushing pellets. They say that the only way to be certain of bringing down the bird is to wait until it has passed over the gun and then fire as it goes away. The result of this strategy, supposedly, is that the shot will enter the unfortunate creature under the edge of its protective coat of feathers.

All this is rubbish, of course, and anyone who has examined a wood pigeon will confirm the softness and fragility of its feathers. In fact they are so loose that some gun dogs will not retrieve them, because they cannot stand the sensation of a mouthful of loose down. The alleged invulnerability of the bird has nothing to do with its plumage, it is simply that the wood pigeon is a master of flight, with eyesight and reactions to match, plus a body which is small enough to present a minute target at the normal range of a shotgun, about 40 yards. When shooters return home with an empty cartridge belt and an empty bag, they may almost be convincing about the 'quist's' bulletproof qualities, but the fact of the matter is that their shot was where the pigeon was not.

Wood pigeon are very good to eat, although unpopular in this country because of their small size and the dark colour of their flesh, but properly prepared in a pie they are food fit for a king and found room on the board of many a royal banquet in the past.

The most common method of shooting pigeons is decoying. The birds, supposedly, are fooled by a collection of wood, rubber or even paper pigeons, arranged in a field in front of a hide wherein sits the shooter. The psychology of this is that the pigeons will think all their comrades are gorging themselves on the crop, and will close their wings and drop in to join the feast, regardless of a fusillade of shots from the waiting guns. Reality is somewhat different.

You sit for three hours or so in a cold hedgerow behind a draughty screen of branches or an even draughtier camouflage net, whilst circulation in the extremities ceases to function and the metal of the gun takes on a hostile degree of coldness. You search the heavens for a sign of the countless pigeons which rose from the crop as you entered the field and winged away into the distant wood on the hill, to watch with fascination as the lifelike pattern of decoy birds is arranged, all head to wind and feeding frantically. Eventually out of a clear sky comes a passing bird who has not been witness to the subterfuge and is mentally deranged enough to consider the rubber birds real. Excitement mounts as the bird sets his wings and starts his glide down to join the decoys. With numb fingers you grip the gun and watch, with a pounding heart, the downward progress of your quarry.

This is the moment when the average sportsman starts to think about allowance for wind and lead, none of which will help when the bird finally comes into range, for as it drops almost to the ground it will be found that a twig, previously considered a vital piece of camouflage, is obscuring the view or catching the end of the barrels.

Ignoring these minor difficulties the gun is raised and fired. The pigeon and twenty-six of his comrades, who were approaching unseen from behind, take fright and beat off out of range, climbing

Estuary birds

like fighters, and the hunter is left to sit and curse. Of course there are
people who can decoy wood pigeons successfully and indeed make a
living from selling them to game dealers. But for the ordinary mortal
the pigeon is a quarry who will outwit him nine times out of ten – a
fact proved by the vast numbers of pigeons to be found in the early
winter on fields of Brussels sprouts or rape. Despite every man's hand
being turned against them they still seem to go forth and multiply.

Our own native flocks of pigeon are supplemented in the winter
months by visitors from Europe, especially the Low Countries, but
the most migration takes place within the confines of these islands,
with birds from the north of England and Scotland moving south in
hard weather.

Other migrants, of course, travel from far afield to reach our shores.
On the estuaries there is a whirr of activity as migrant waders en route
from the Arctic skim over the glistening mud. The first of the winter
duck plane in to land on the Wash marshes, vanguard of the thousands
who will follow on the north winds. Unfortunately, many planners of
roads and public works seem to regard estuaries and mudflats as a
challenge to be overcome. Ever since Mr Vermuden drained the fens
of East Anglia, there has been a concerted and, some say, misguided
effort to rid our countryside of wetlands despite the fact that fenland
and estuarine habitat is vital to many of our wild creatures.

Estuaries have a bad public image. Some of our greatest writers,
especially Charles Dickens with *Great Expectations* and Conan Doyle
with his Sherlock Holmes stories, have set their more menacing scenes

49

in and around estuaries and marshes. If either of these writers wished to suggest a setting for 'dirty doings' all they had to do was to describe an estuary, with muddy gullies, wreathing mists and treacherous sands. Until today there has been little or no outcry when an estuary has been chosen for a rubbish tip or when fenland has been drained.

Yet estuaries in winter are magic places, orchestrated with the fluting of thousands of waders as they dash and scurry like clockwork toys over the glistening mud down at the tideline. Curlew yodel in to land, and thrust their curved bills into the rich mud. Shelduck slurp and sift the soupy water at the tide's edge, filtering minute snails from the ooze with tip-tilted bills, and beneath the water, brackish and frothy, is a world unique in its structure.

The changing salinity and varied aeration of estuarine waters provides a home for a host of both sea and fresh water creatures, creatures who have adapted to survive the tide leaving their home high and dry twice a day and exposing them to the elements and myriad predators. An estuary in fact looks like one of the most potentially hostile habitats a creature could find itself in. In an area where the temperature and chemical composition of the water are ever-changing, it is not hard to imagine what havoc the hand of man can wreak. Even the simple act of dredging a channel for shipping can cause untold damage. Draining the mud kills its inhabitants, the small worms and crustaceans, and it is on these lower organisms that the birds and higher forms of life depend.

The ecology of wetlands is finely balanced, more so than that of any other habitat. Wetlands are immensely fertile because the inrush of sea water brings food to the mudflats, as does the fresh water of the river, to a lesser degree, feeding the estuary from the landward side.

It is not only interference with the estuary itself which can upset this

Tubeworms

Shovellers in winter on the River Gade at Water End, Hertfordshire

delicate balance. Inland the preoccupation with keeping land dry causes river boards to want to turn all winding, quiet-flowing rivers into canals, straightening out the natural bends and oxbows, turning the river into a channel solely as a means to get the water to the sea as quickly as possible.

The practice of extensive field drainage has led to a variety of problems, especially where artificial fertilisers are widely used. These are deemed necessary to obtain high yields from marginal land, but they are highly concentrated, unlike organic fertilisers, and tend to be washed down into the subsoil by rain and thence by field drainage into the river system. The net result is that the plant life of the river receives far more nutrition than it needs and the plants produce more growth than normal along the whole course of the river until the estuary is reached.

Under normal circumstances the water reaching the mouth of a river would have a relatively low level of plant nutrients, for these would have been taken out by plants further upstream. Most plant food would normally be supplied from the seaward side of the ecosystem. The result of the artificial imbalance is an explosion of lower plant organisms such as algae which cover and choke the mud and its inhabitants.

Once part of the food chain dies, the whole system collapses like a pack of cards, for all things in an estuary are interdependent. Without the worms who live in the mud, the birds and fish are deprived of food and leave. Birds, especially, cannot cope. Dunlins and curlews would never be seen on a bird table for their feeding requirements are too specialised. When the estuaries are completely polluted the birds will be gone forever. At this very moment, all over the country, plans are under consideration for marshland reclamation and for marinas and industry on tidal flats.

An example of one which has already gone under the dead hand of the reclaimer is the small mouth of the river Teign which runs from the old market town of Newton Abbot in Devon. Here the tidal flats have been infilled for development at the top end of the river and a bypass bridge bisects the river itself. Once, not long ago, this marsh-land was home to vast packs of wintering duck, so vast that they were hunted by punt gunners, intrepid men who ignored the elements, creeping out in the winter dawn to bring their long guns to bear on the duck.

Now the duck are gone and the last punt-gunner's boat lies like a stranded shark its long lines half-submerged in the mud. Holes in its

Gun punt

sides bear witness to its redundancy. It is almost in the shadow of the new road bridge, a symbol of destruction, old and new style.

However, all is not blackness and gloom on this front for in the past ten years awareness of our need to protect our wetland environments has increased, and there are estuarine habitats on busy rivers which the planners have left relatively unspoiled. One which springs to mind is on the Exe, in Devon again. Between the town of Exmouth and the railway (a stretch that long ago was the atmospheric railway, brainchild of that king of engineers Isambard Kingdom Brunel), is a leaden expanse of water and mud bounded on its seaward side by the sand dunes of Dawlish Warren.

Brent goose

During the summer holiday season this area plays host to thousands of human visitors, but in winter it is the landfall and refuge of dark-breasted brent geese. Skeins of these beautiful geese beat in, singing their wild songs, from the wastes of Siberia where they breed. December sees them beating upwind, calling like a pack of hounds in full cry, as they crest the marram-topped sand dunes and whiffle in to land on the grey water like dark snowflakes.

Further up the estuary where the parkland of Powderham Castle almost reaches the tideline, huge flocks of grey plover carpet the water meadow, each bird balanced on one leg, head beneath grey wing, as they wait for the receding water to uncover their feeding grounds. On the mudbanks in the middle of the river, bar-tailed godwits stride the silt on stilt-like legs, probing with knitting-needle bills in search of the lugworm deep in his burrow in the ooze. Redshank 'pleup' along the margin, marching like a platoon of well-drilled soldiers.

As the tide recedes the glistening mud is criss-crossed with thousands of tiny arrowhead footprints made by knot and sanderlings, who peep and pipe across the flats in a relentless search for food before the rising tide closes the restaurant. In the shallow pools lone avocets sweep their sailmaker's-needle beaks from side to side, reaping minute crustaceans from the soupy water.

Suddenly this feeding, scurrying, tightly knit community is thrown into panic and the air is full of shrill cries and flickering wings. A wintering peregrine falcon sweeps down the estuary like a feathered arrow. With a thud and a burst of grey feathers the falcon detaches a grey plover from the wheeling flocks and skids round in the cold clear air to catch it before its lifeless body hits the water. Then the falcon swings away on the wind like a trapeze artist, the plover clutched in its talons. Quickly and quietly the life of the estuary returns to the important business of feeding.

Peregrine

That scene happened on the Exe, though it could have been Morecambe Bay or the Wash: but for how much longer?

The clock of the year is slowly winding down as December progresses, and the feverish activity of the human world is counterbalanced by a period of equally marked inactivity in the natural world.

Insects and hibernating animals are settling to the business of surviving the expected cold of the next three months. The hedgehogs are wrapped in a blanket of dead leaves, their pointed faces pressed into the softness of their under-fur. All their processes are slowing down and the temperature of their spine-covered bodies is barely above that of the surrounding air, their breathing and heartbeat almost imperceptible. The hedgehog is rather low in the order of mammals; he could almost be described as a prototype which nature decided to keep when the new models were being designed.

Marsupial mammals, pouched animals whose young are born when they are at an early stage in their development, were superseded by the more advanced placental mammals. The first of these was very similar in bodily construction to the hedgehog, though fossil records do not tell us whether or not these shrew-like creatures had spines or fur. Their hibernating instinct and ability to lay down fat have enabled the family of the hedgehog to succeed. It is hard to imagine the snuffling urchin who bumbles around the garden of many suburban homes as a living fossil, but that is what he is.

The hedgehog's near cousin the shrew does not share the ability to shut up shop for the winter, for it has a metabolism so rapid that a day without food would mean certain death by starvation. All day long the

Common shrew

shrew's flexible nose probes and quests in the dead litter, seeking worms and resting insects to satisfy its insatiable appetite.

Because of its constant demand for protein it has, for so small a creature, a very large territory and a temper to match. When two shrews meet then theirs is a world-class match; each minute protagonist squares up to his opponent and verbal abuse is an important part of this serious contest.

Territorial fights are usually games of bluff and counter-bluff, but shrews fight in earnest and it is not uncommon to hear their shrill chatter, or to find the dead of these conflicts in the grass at your feet. On reflection it is easy to understand why shrews are so pugnacious, for with an appetite such as theirs to satisfy, too many shrews in one territory would spell certain death.

The pygmy shrew is the smallest British mammal, weighing only a fraction of an ounce and measuring a mere $2\frac{1}{4}$ in including tail, but what it lacks in size it makes up for in activity and spirit. A wolf-size pygmy shrew or, for that matter, any wolf-sized shrew, would indeed be terrifying!

Another cousin, the mole, is also blessed or cursed, depending on your point of view and the quality of your lawn, with a more than healthy appetite, and like all members of this group the 'gentleman in black velvet' has a regular pattern of sleep and activity – so regular that having found out when a mole is active in a certain area you can revisit that area at four-hourly intervals and be able to tell, almost to the minute, when he will start to forage in the underground tunnels which are his home. The mole is a prodigious tunneller, as those of you who have had a garden devastated overnight will testify.

These tunnels are excavated outwards from the nest, a short distance below the surface, in a roughly rectangular pattern, starting from a flowerbed or a wall or bank. The mole hills are formed from the loose earth thrown up by the tunnelling operations and are not nests as some people imagine. The sleeping quarters are constructed in a bank and are larger than the usual hill, the chamber being lined with dead roots and dry grass.

Like shrews, moles are solitary creatures except in the breeding season and then the sexes only tolerate one another for the brief mating period, after which they separate to get down to the serious business of feeding. The young are born in the spring, blind and helpless, in a specially constructed breeding chamber and after five weeks of maternal care they are out on their own to fend for themselves.

As a burrowing machine the mole is unmatched, from the tip of his questing nose with its mass of sensory hairs to the end of his ridiculous tail. He is the perfect excavator, for nature has equipped him with front paws which are broad and wide and hairless, outward-pointing and furnished with strong nails, actuated by a set of shoulder muscles which would make a world-class weightlifter green with envy. His coat has also been expressly evolved for life in a tube. It stands up like velvet straight from the skin, dense and silky, able to stand being brushed in any direction while still retaining its density and dust-proof qualities.

It was this coat that in the past made the mole a valuable commercial proposition. Not only was it good for hats and waistcoats, it was supreme as a plumber's 'joint wiper'. In the days when most water pipes were made from lead they had to be joined with a bulbous solder joint and this had to be 'wiped', that is, made into a smooth uniform tapering 'egg' of solder between the two ends of the joined pipes. This was performed while the solder on the pipe was just molten and the joint was shaped by the moleskin held in the palm of the hand. The dense fur and the relatively thick skin smoothed the surface of the join and protected the hand from the heat of the solder. But with the advent of copper pipe and mechanical joints the use of moleskin became unnecessary and the mole catcher rapidly became a thing of the past.

In my Devon childhood the mole catcher was a very real person, craggy, quiet and immensely skilful at his craft. Cecil, as he was called,

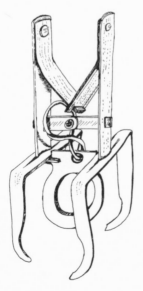

Mole trap

taught me that the mole is extremely sensitive to vibration through the soil and a clumsy footfall would cause the little miner to cease operations and head home to safety. Cecil rarely used mole traps; his method was to watch for the telltale movement in the turf and catch the mole by stamping on the run behind it and digging it out with his hand. It took me many months to master his technique and with my light weight, unless the mole was burrowing close to the surface, I was unable to crush the tunnel, I quickly found that it was wise to ascertain in which direction the mole was facing, as his front end is fitted with a great number of very sharp pointed teeth.

My elder brother Don was the proud possessor of a string of mole traps, metal spring devices which resembled pliers with the jaws crossed. These traps were intended to be placed in an active mole run and were triggered to close by a flat spring when the mole pushed the trigger plate. Providing an active run could be found these were most effective and unlike most traps of that period they did kill the animal instantly and humanely. In consequence, our garden shed was decorated, if that is not too grisly a term, with the square shapes of many mole skins nailed onto its blistered paint surface, drying prior to being sent off to the mole-skin dealers. As I remember it they fetched half a crown for ten which was a valuable addition to our pocket money.

With the advent of copper pipe and the demise of the 'wiped' joint there should have been a veritable explosion of moles in the late 1950s and early 1960s, but this was not to be, for agriculture had begun the changes which led to modern intensive farming with its dependence on chemicals.

The mole is at the top of a food chain among ground-living animals. The organic chlorine and phosphorous insecticides build up in its prey and in turn in the fat of the mole's own body. When food is scarce, which for a mole could be after ten hours, the fat is reabsorbed and along with it the insecticide, now highly concentrated. This is fatal for the mole. 'Moley' is making a comeback, but it is unlikely that he will ever be as common as he was in my childhood.

The celebration of Christmas has greatly changed although not so much in the country as in the towns. Friendliness, however, still pervades the long dark evenings, with neighbours ignoring the services of Her Majesty's Post Office to deliver Christmas cards and presents by hand. This is not necessarily a good thing from the safety point of view, for it is difficult to refuse to have a drink with all your friends and by the time you have visited the fifth or sixth house the prospect of driving home looms menacingly. Although such an efficient means of transport, the motor car is far less forgiving of the occasional mistake than were the Dartmoor ponies which constituted the usual means of travel around the more inaccessible Devon villages of the 1940s.

The wartime shortage of petrol forced most people to use 'Shanks's pony', horseback or tractor. Bicycles in that part of North Devon were not really a practical proposition for there were few miles of roadway which did not slope steeply up or down. The slaty limestone which composed the bed rock of the area was originally laid down in the upper palaeozoic era of the earth's development and in the 350 million years or so between then and now the surface of the earth has wrinkled like the crust on clotted cream, buckling as it cooled.

The policeman and the midwife were two people who did use a bicycle, more as part of their stock-in-trade than for speed; the policeman's bike especially had a bare polished patch of metal on its sturdy crossbar where generations of village bobbies had gripped it as they pushed it up Bratton Hill.

Walking was the usual way of getting about for everyone and it was not unknown for farmers to walk the eight and a half miles into Okehampton market driving their plodding red Devon cattle before them, then when the sale was over, to walk back, sometimes with four or five pigs. The pigs were sober enough, but the intake of scrumpy made the steering and judgement of their drovers somewhat cloudy, and sometimes a disconsolate pig could be seen wandering down the main street of the village whilst its owner slept in a hedge three miles 'back along'.

Ownership of an animal was easy enough to determine. As only four people had left the village to go to market that morning and three had already made it back to the inn, there was little doubt as to who owned the pig. All that was needed was a temporary home for the animal until the owner claimed it.

Most people in the village kept a pig either officially or unofficially, for at that time there were strict rules about food production and 'black market' were dirty words used with disgust by honest folk as they heaved the swill into the trough for their unofficial pigs. My father, a civilian employed on rescue services in nearby Plymouth, joined in this rural sport of rearing a pig, but being an entrepreneur at heart he would not settle for the runt of the litter (a piglet too small to survive, or so the Ministry of Food was persuaded to believe). We possessed three Wessex saddlebacks, beautiful piglets with benign expressions and happy dispositions.

The unofficial pigsty

These animals sometimes resided in the garage across the road. This was a wooden structure which had first seen the light of day many centuries before the motor car had even been considered and had been in turn cow byre or shippon, stable and village swede store, before being elevated as accommodation for the horseless carriage. Because of its chequered past the garage was predisposed to the accommodation of animals, all the feeding troughs still being *in situ*; it was the natural place to put unofficial pigs.

However, our beautiful saddlebacks were not content to remain unofficial and due to the antiquity of the garage, its ability to contain three rather inquisitive piglets was somewhat impaired. In consequence there was a constant queue of callers to tell my mother that 'they pigs be out again missus'. Then it was all hands to the pump as the animals were recovered from wherever they had wandered, and there were times when even the local policeman could be seen driving the unofficial pigs back home to their sty. I was not privy to the discussion as to the division of the carcasses when our saddlebacks met their end, but no doubt the bobby found a parcel of ribs, and scraps for his dog, on his back doorstep.

In this wild area the horse provided a means of transport unequalled in its effectiveness in the hilly and rather muddy countryside. Each autumn the ponies would be driven from their moorland home to be marked for ownership, and this still takes place. Many would be returned for the winter, but a certain number would be sold to be broken for the saddle or as draught animals. Dartmoors make good, if unpredictable, saddle horses; they are very strong and incredibly hardy with an excellent turn of speed, and it is this speed and their acceleration up hill which has led to many unwary riders being unseated when something has spooked the pony into flight. But well broken and at about five years of age they are model transport, especially for the regular inebriate.

A local character used to visit the village inn on a Saturday night when he would proceed to drink rough cider until he could hold no more. This once-weekly task successfully accomplished, he would be placed with care on the back of his faithful Dartmoor and the pony would unfailingly take him home, where he would gently fall from the saddle outside his farmhouse door to be helped inside by his disapproving wife.

The pony meanwhile would take itself to the stable and, because it was not wearing a bit, a piece of rope serving for a bridle and a blanket for a saddle, it proceeded to feed and water itself from the manger until its owner came to take it out on the farm rounds in the morning. This friendship between man and horse continued until both were in their dotage.

The last type of transport, the tractor, was virtually useless for its original purpose on the high and glutinous land, where the heavy horse was the best and safest method of ploughing. But the village did boast two tractors and these were mainly pressed reluctantly into service to take the farmers and their children to church on Sunday morning. The wife and children sat on the trailer attired in Sunday best whilst the farmer, in a dark shiny suit, attempted to protect his white, throat-cutting collar from the clouds of oily smoke which belched from the exhaust pipe of the paraffin-burning engine as it wheezed asthmatically up the hill to the church.

Because of fuel shortages all tractors were fitted with a system of carburation which employed petrol to start the engine and then switched to TVO (tractor vapourising oil) when it warmed up. The changeover was always traumatic as the engine went into paroxysms of coughing accompanied by black smoke rings and soot from the unsilenced exhaust pipe.

Creature comforts on these tractors were painfully few, and they were men of iron who sat for hours upon the perforated steel saddle-shaped driving seat. This was fixed to the gearbox housing by a massive steel spring and all of the imperfections and vibrations were transmitted to the driver's spine via the iron-shod road wheels. The one thing the tractor could do better than the heavy horse was to drive the pulleys on a box thresher.

In spite of wartime shortages, Christmas was still a time for good eating and opening presents, for church services, choirs and carols and a constant stream of visitors. I was used to visitors, for our home supplied the room which the doctor used for his surgery and dispensary when he visited the village twice a week. But at Christmas the visitors were different and invariably affectionately merry, for the locals had their own cider press. The cloudy amber brew was drunk with relish, so much so that many of the male members of the community would pass the festival in hazy enjoyment only to be stunned back into reality by the traditional pastime of the 'Hunt' and the 'Boxing Day Shoot'.

The Hunt carried on, though in the absence of the younger members of the community who were away serving their country, it was a motley group which assembled. The foxes were in little danger for they had ample cover in the dense hedgerows and only suicidal or geriatric animals ever succumbed. But it was a tradition and a spectacle and many of the villagers turned out as followers.

The Shoot was a slightly different matter, for everything shot was supplementary to the diet. The haze of rough cider left over from the preceding celebrations made the usually good marksmanship flexible, however, and a rabbit breaking across the line of the guns presented a real danger of perforated knees as guns were waved wildly in all directions.

The choice of guns and ammunition was, to say the least, variable. Many of the arms in use were hammer guns dating from the previous century and had had little or no contact with a gunsmith since they were new, subsequent work having been carried out by the local blacksmith. This showed clearly in the profusion of brazed patchwork on barrels, crude hammers and the standard binding of broken stocks with iron rods and copper wire.

It was not only the guns which had individuality. The ammunition varied from standard twelve-bore shells, hoarded over the years, to brass-cased monsters emblazoned with a broad arrow, apparently for shooting German parachutists. A demonstration of the power of the

Lapwing

charge from these monsters and the destructive force of the single lead ball had to be seen to be believed – it would sever an ash sapling 10 in or so in diameter.

Considering the savage recoil of the gun the marksmanship would have had to be remarkable and it was fortunate for us that the German Parachute Corps were not called upon to drop over that part of Devon. How many of these rounds the average farm gun could have taken before the barrels burst is a matter for conjecture.

There can be little comparison with a modern Boxing-day Shoot, where the sportsmen are well equipped with expensive guns, or the Meet of horse and hounds with the immaculately turned-out members of the local pony club, but I doubt whether the enjoyment is quite so keen now, because then no one was out to impress anybody. Times have changed.

The year has come to an end and in the remaining water meadows snipe are arriving in increasing numbers to probe in the soft earth for grubs and worms, and lapwings fly in to rest on the frost-covered pasture, their wispy feathers blown about by the cold northerly winds. Winter is making its presence felt on the land. Back in the shelter of the Dorset downlands, the Dorset Horn sheep are already giving birth, vanguard of the coming lambing season.

4
JANUARY

With the coming of the new year the quiet period continues for the dwellers in the hedge bottom and woodlands. In the dry dead wood of the fallen frost-rimed beeches, the caterpillars of the goat moth, so called because the larvae have a smell reminiscent of a billy goat, munch the pulpy timber. They are in no hurry, for their home is their larder and even though they have a larval stage of up to four years before the damask-grey patterned moth emerges there is no danger they will run out of food.

In the beech trunk other forces are at work on the close-grained timber; threads of fungus creep along the sap tubes to dissolve and soften the wood, all part of the process which nature has devised to return to the earth that which has been drawn from it.

This century will go down in the history of man as the time when trees were taken from the landscape more quickly than at any other period. At the beginning of the century the 'war to end all wars' caused trees to be stripped from the land like corn from the field at harvest time; and more recently the disaster of Dutch elm disease has spread like wildfire from a small beginning on the east coast, until the elm is in danger of becoming only an image enshrined in the paintings of John Constable.

The demise of these noble trees has marked the end of an era in the

English landscape, for the elm, with its familiar inverted-triangle shape and twisted filigree of branches, was one of the commonest trees in the declining hedgerow scenery. Elms were planted by our forefathers as boundary markers and for their wood: the tightly interlocked grain is the perfect material for articles which have to withstand great stress.

Elm has been mentioned briefly in a previous chapter as the timber used for farm carts and waggon-hubs, where its strength and resistance to cracking were tested to the limit. As well as strength, wet elm has a resistance to rot second only to oak and elm timber immersed in water and buried underground keeps for thousands of years. Recent excavations in the City of London uncovered Roman water pipes, buried in the clay, which were made from whole logs hollowed out; despite their age the wood was still clearly recognisable as elm. It was, and to a lesser extent still is, the prime timber for making coffins.

The wild grain of elm makes it very difficult to work; nevertheless it is often used for furniture, and in particular for chairs because of its resistance to strain and cracking; the famous 'Windsor chair' was founded on elm seat blocks.

Dutch elm disease has caused millions of trees to be felled, but unfortunately much of the wood is valueless for furniture making. Also, unless carefully prepared and seasoned it will twist and warp out of shape within a few years. The old furniture makers used this characteristic to their benefit by laying together planks with opposing grains, the warping and stress of one plank being balanced against the stress of the opposing plank, thereby keeping the equilibrium.

The home of English country furniture-making is now, as it was a hundred years ago, the Chiltern town of High Wycombe, which nestles in a valley in the chalk downland. The hills rising above the town are clothed with thick beech woodland and it was here at the end of the nineteenth century that the 'chair bodgers' plied their trade, turning the spindles of the chair on primitive, but remarkably efficient, lathes which used the spring power of a sapling bent to turn the spindle of the lathe. One family concern still produces elm and beech furniture there, although modern technology is now used and not the bodgers' pole lathe.

The decline of the elm means not only a greatly changed countryside; it means that the universe of creatures for which the elm was the hub has also ceased to exist and comparatively common creatures and insects are now becoming rare. For instance, butterflies like the delicate white-letter hairstreak, so called because of the white W which adorns the underwing, are now almost extinct in areas where once they were widespread. This small butterfly can survive on wych-elm, but sadly that too is affected; the scolitis beetle attacks the smoother bark of the wych-elm too, spreading the fungus which will block the life-giving sap. Unless a miracle happens the 'white letter' is doomed to virtual extinction.

Another and far more spectacular insect which feeds on elm leaves is the rare large tortoiseshell butterfly. This insect has always been local in its distribution, but since the turn of the century it has declined to the verge of extinction and its days as a British species must be numbered.

What of all the elm which has been felled and left in the fields? Much of this will be used as fuel in grates and wood-burning stoves, where its wonderful grain will end up as ashes. We should mourn the passing of the elms and thank heaven we have been privileged to enjoy the sight of them in their prime.

The creatures that depend on dead timber will of course have a field day. Woodboring insects find abundant forage on dead elms and those birds and animals which prey upon them in turn increase, taking advantage of the bonanza. In the January cold even woodpeckers can be seen, sometimes in built-up areas, jerking upwards on the rough bark searching for insects. Also the tiny mouse-like tree creeper is more numerous because of the elm tragedy. So nature has been able to come to terms with the devastation and turn it to her advantage.

January is a month when Britain is likely to come under the influence of cold winds from northern Europe, and these carry the snow for the first deep rich covering, causing chaos to communications but beautifying the drabbest urban landscape. Some of the northern counties, of course, have already had a considerable amount and the last couple of winters have seen much heavier January falls in the West Country.

A whole new world is with us in snowy weather, for with the glitter of white fields and branches appear the wanderers of the bird world. Depending on the length and severity of the cold spell they come from all over, for as far as the birds are concerned there has always been a Common Market and they know no boundaries.

Because of our position in the northern hemisphere, close to a major land mass and yet surrounded by warm sea, our climate is generally milder than that of our neighbours on the continent of Europe and in Scandinavia, and therefore we become the refuge for a considerable number of winter migrants. The thrushes, redwings and fieldfares fill

Waxwings

our dull winter days with their calls, but there are other migrants such as the spectacular waxwing, a finch-like bird from the far northern pine forests with salmon-pink plumage and a crest of feathers on its head. The waxy tips to its wing feathers which look like a number of red 'Vesta' matches tucked in give the bird its name. These elegant birds appear during January, fanning out from their home territory, Finland. They feed on berries, especially rowan (mountain ash), and their irregular migrations may have something to do with the failure of the rowan to fruit in their own countries, or may just reflect a population explosion, forcing them to look further afield. Whatever their cause, 'waxwing winters', when the birds appear in vast numbers on the eastern seaboard of England and Scotland, occur periodically and because the bird is so spectacular their arrival seldom goes unnoticed.

There are records of 'waxwing' years from as far back as the fifteenth century and in recent times the winters of 1956–60 produced record numbers of these birds. Being as large as starlings and with appetites to match, the waxwings soon exhaust the few berries left for them by the earlier visitors, so often they turn up in suburban gardens, eating the berries from ornamental shrubs such as cotoneaster. They have not been recorded as breeding in Great Britain. It seems likely that those we see during winter irruptions are in excess of the normal population, and sadly, as is usual in these cases, most will not return to their native lands but will die on migration.

There are other visitors who will return to the far north to breed and come back here again year after year as long as there is suitable habitat for them. These are the wildfowl – ducks, geese and swans – which flock to our shores. They move ahead of the bad weather, from the lochs and estuaries of Scotland to the reservoirs of the south-east and often as far south as the Cornish rivermouths.

Wildfowl are the most stirring of birds for many of us, for they are free wild travellers constantly moving over immense distances. They are creatures of mythology and legend and the sight and sound of them evokes the same emotions as listening to a Beethoven symphony. It was wildfowl which first kindled in me the desire to make my living, as well as my life, with the natural world. Having from early days wanted to be a professional naturalist, it was not until, during one of my family's wanderings, we came to rest temporarily in Chiswick that the obsession took a definite direction. At the age of fourteen in an urban environment I was like a fish out of water, wandering aimlessly in suburban parks and slouching up and down the banks of the polluted Thames attempting to alleviate homesickness for the countryside. One day a schoolfriend told me about the 'ressies' and that was it. I discovered Barn Elms, a complex of reservoirs on the Putney side of the Thames. Many happy hours were spent there and one particular morning in January was a turning point.

By good fortune I avoided the reservoir keeper, gained unchallenged access and walked against the wind along the causeway which formed the centre bank of the reservoirs, scanning the water avidly, not for anything in particular, but more to reinforce the pleasant sensation of being alone with the wind and water and wild things.

A small white bird caught my attention. It bobbed on the surface buoyantly like a snowflake and even with inadequate fieldglasses I could see that it was a duck, but what a duck! Snow-white with a black patch around the eye, a black-lined crest and a thin line of black on its

Male smew

snowy side: it was a smew, although I had to wait until I arrived home, breathless, to identify it. Smew are one of the most beautiful of the whole family of fish-eating sawbilled ducks. From that moment on I was hooked on wildfowl. Every spare minute during that January and the following months was spent at Barn Elms until finally the reservoir keeper caught up with me. 'And what do you think you are doing?' he demanded with mock severity. 'Birdwatching,' I replied innocently and before he had a chance to inform me that because of safety regulations children were not allowed near the reservoirs unaccompanied, I launched into a description of all the ducks I had seen past and present.

I don't think I paused for breath until half the list of British birds, actual and potential, had been covered. In a brief pause at the end of my discourse he delivered the speech about children and safety, but without much conviction; he knew he was dealing with a hard case and kindly realised it would be better to know where I was and give in; the infection was too far advanced for a cure. With or without his permission I would somehow get in to the reservoir. 'Right Lad,' he said, 'you can come in, but you must tell me when you arrive and when you leave so I know you are safe.'

This action, which could have cost him his job had I drowned, was incredibly kind and understanding and his patience in putting up with a stream of undoubtedly irritating questions was remarkable. Although I never knew him by any other name than 'Sir', I am indebted to him.

That long-ago winter passed and the smew left. I watched through the summer months with impatience, just praying for the winter to come again and when it finally did come I was the proud possessor of a Dolland four-draw telescope, a masterpiece of brass and red leather.

This had been bought for £3, money carefully collected by working, scheming, begging and borrowing, and for Christmas that year my parents presented me with a pair of Barr and Stroud prismatic binoculars, ex-WD as was all optical equipment then available. With this outfit I was well equipped to study the world's wildfowl and through the first weeks of the year avidly scanned the leaden water for the first smew. When it came I did not need my glasses to know it was there on the water like an ice fairy, but with the new telescope I could pick out the delicate pencilling which adorns the bird's breast and sides and also identify the female smew, the red head as fine and delicate as her mate's but lacking the white brilliance.

The telescope also brought to life the beauty of the other ducks, goosanders, large relatives of the smew with green heads and pink sides, the tiny teal and the widgeon who sat on the surface in large flocks, their 'wheooo' call carrying thrillingly on the icy wind.

Just after the war there were very few birdwatchers, but one thing they all had in common was a willingness to listen and to give advice and help with identification. Some of them were less tolerant than others, but all must have been relieved when the flow of questions ceased. One man in particular was to have a far more profound effect on my life than almost any other before or since, and his help in providing an introduction to the Royal Society for the Protection of Birds was invaluable. This quiet and rather gentle man was Viscount Alanbrooke, Field-Marshal and Chief of Imperial General Staff during

Teal

the Second World War. We would walk together on Barn Elms discussing bird life and the natural-history scene, and he would listen patiently to my misidentifications and correct them in such a way that I did not lose confidence in my ability. Regrettably I did not see him again after joining the RSPB at their offices in Ecclestone Square, Victoria, and never had the chance to thank him, but perhaps he would not have minded. He would have been satisfied in the knowledge that he had enabled someone else to share his interest in the natural world. That interest in wildfowl firmly took root and I still look forward to winter and the arrival of the first winter visitors.

My present home in the Chilterns is on a flyway, an aerial corridor down which passes a multitude of overwintering ducks, geese and swans, and at the beginning of the year, if the ponds and reservoirs are not frozen over, the early morning sky is filled with skeins of waterfowl flying high like dots along the track of the Grand Union Canal, stopping off at various reservoirs which feed the canal.

Tring reservoir's National Nature Reserve in Hertfordshire is one of these and is recognised as a wildfowl area of special importance by the Nature Conservancy Council. I have been an honorary warden of the reserve at Tring for many years, and such reserves do a lot of good work: but how sad it is that we need nature reserves at all. What a reflection on modern man that he makes the countryside so hostile to wild creatures that we have to set aside special areas where they can have peace and a chance to survive.

To the naturalist, snow is as useful a clue as is the murder weapon to the detective: it confirms his suspicions. Even tiny children love to go tracking in the snow, and what a tale the first all-covering page of white crystals has to impart to the keen observer. Arrowhead footprints of birds hopping disconsolately in an unfamiliar world, the tiny scurried tracks of mice in the hedge-bottom and the paired snow-shoes of rabbits wintersporting at the field's edge, foxtracks, precise and elegant in a straight purposeful line across the damask-white, blue-edged tracks which tell the story of the previous night's hunting.

The tracks show the circuitous stalk towards a patch of disturbed snow where a rabbit had been feeding, the rabbit's dash to cover when it spotted the hunter and an orange stain where the disgusted fox marked his territory in frustration, before stepping on to seek out pheasants roosting in the holly trees. Did he hope that one bird, perhaps pricked in the last shoot, would fall to provide an easy meal for the 'picker up' in the red fur coat?

The tracks sometimes tell another story, a love story. For at this

71

Rabbit footprints in the snow; clues for the nature detective

time of year reynard has more than food on his mind, and the strongly scented territory-marks he leaves are his calling card.

January is the month when foxes mate, with the dog fox singing his love song to the vixen in a nearby wood; soon her tracks are dancing and weaving around his. Here and there in the snow is the impression of the vixen's body where she yittered in the appeasement posture to the dog fox. Then, formalities over and the engagement agreed, parallel tracks make off across the snow.

Such is our climate that no sooner is the countryside covered with white than – usually – the weather pattern shifts and a thaw sets in. Then in the southern woodlands, the winter aconite flowers, resembling green-white remnants of the snow, and snowdrops push up their sword-shaped leaves into the weak sunshine. For all the disruption it causes, melting snow is good for the land. There is an old country saying that a foot of snow is worth an inch of rain and the truth of this is obvious if you give it some thought. Unlike rain, which tends to saturate the upper layer of the earth quickly, then run off the surface and away into ditches and so to rivers carrying with it some of the goodness of the soil, snow as it melts drips into the soil slowly and percolates down into the subsoil. The process is so slow that most of the melt-water finds its way into the underground water system, a maze of streams and rivers flowing along the underworld of the land. Its penetration is limited only by the subsoil, the structure of the bedrock and the underlying strata.

In the Chilterns and South Downs the chalk holds large quantities of water which is constantly being fed down into underground rivers which flow through gravel bands over the impervious bedrock. On the surface these watersheds are marked by dry valleys, but in places, where the bedrock is close to the surface, the subterranean streams rise up as bubbly springs and form the famous chalk streams of this area. In the chalk downlands, too, are phenomena known as bournes, streams which appear and disappear seasonally. But springs and bournes have several things in common, the purity and clarity of the water caused by filtering through chalk, the highly alkaline Ph of the water and the constant temperature. Because of these three factors the water of chalk streams is rich in plant, insect and fish life. The best trout fishing to be had in England is in the chalk streams of the south, such as the Test and the Itchen which are justly famous for their mighty trout.

It is at this time of year that brown trout spawn. The hen fish gather at the 'redds', the spawning ground, and each hollows out a 'nest' for the eggs by beating the gravel with its fins and the sides of its body.

When the male fish joins the female at the redds, in an ecstasy of shivering fins and gaping mouths, both fish deposit their contribution to the next generation. The female covers the vulnerable ova and leaves them to hatch in the well-oxygenated gravel. The round golden eggs rest for six weeks in this watery nursery before they hatch and their parents, fins frayed, drop back downstream to rest in quiet eddies and feed themselves back into condition for the coming spring.

The increase in popularity of fishing in our rivers and streams has led to the introduction of the rainbow trout, a North American import, which displays many of the fighting qualities of the seatrout. In normal circumstances the rainbow does not spawn in the rivers into which it has been introduced. However, there are exceptions to every rule and in the Chess in Hertfordshire, and one other river nearby, they have done so, and it is a marvellous sight to see the red-sided, dark-bodied males and the deep silver females side by side on the gravel of the clear streams.

The progeny of this spawning seem apparently to revert to one of the sub-species of the crossing and river-spawned fish are usually very much brighter in colour than their parents: the rainbow band on the fishes' sides is a real rainbow, not the shadow of colour which is found in 'stew'-bred fish. Whether this colour difference is really a reversion to type or whether it is just that, in the more competitive situation of a river, fish are simply healthier and better fitted for survival, we do not know; but whatever the reason the brightly colour-banded fish are a joy to catch on rod and line.

Other types of fish occupy the angler in these cold winter months, and the canals and rivers and lakes are decorated with the umbrellas of the coarse-fish anglers. The term 'coarse' is an anomaly, the only difference between the two types of fishing is that they have different close seasons and in the case of coarse fishing the catch is usually returned to the water. This is not so in game fishing. Trout and salmon are killed for the pot. Yet coarse fish are reasonably good to eat, and perch, pike and carp are thought by some to be as good as trout. In fact pike is justly a delicacy in almost every country except Great Britain. A 'jack' or young pike of up to 8 lb, flavoured with basil, steamed and cooled, served with a salad and mayonnaise, is as ambrosia to the gods.

Pike fishing is a sport for the hardy, for now the females are at their best, full-conditioned and deep-bellied, lying like submarines in the remnants of the weedbed, wound up like springs and armed with a mouthful of teeth like grapples all facing back towards the throat, just waiting to speed from their hiding places to snap up passing roach.

Pike

The pike is a fish of legend, a marauder, wolf of the pond, and many children have embarked on a lifetime of fishing having first been enthralled by tales of 'that great pike' lurking under the lilies of the local lake. Although pike grow to immense size – indeed fish of over 60 lb have been recorded – such monsters are exceptional, the average fish being nearer 8 lb. Even so, on light tackle a pike is a worthy adversary.

The practice of live baiting for pike has largely gone, fortunately so, for it required the fisherman to impale a living fish on one barb of a treble hook suspended beneath a cork float. This was termed a 'bung' and after being cast to a likely spot in the water the hapless tethered fish struggled beneath the bung providing a tempting meal for pike who were attracted by its agony. As a means of fishing it was exceptionally successful, but as a way of treating a living creature it was barbarous. Fortunately a band of fishermen who titled themselves specimen hunters, dedicated and knowledgeable souls, discovered that large pike will sooner eat dead fish than chase live ones, so dead baiting has become the more usual way to attract and hook them.

A dead fish, usually a herring, is set upon the end of a free-running line without either weights or float, liberally embellished with an array of treble hooks. The bait is then cast and the line left to run free from the reel. Because the fixed-spool reel is an essential part of the pike fisher's equipment the bale arm is left open, so that when the pike takes the dead bait it is free to move away from the spot without feeling the resistance of the line. At the rod there is an indicator, either a piece of silver paper or an electrically operated buzzer, which tells the angler that a pike has picked up the bait.

At this point, when the fish has had time to turn the dead bait prior to swallowing it, the bale arm is closed and the treble hooks are set by striking hard with the rod. A pike's mouth is hard and it needs a hefty pull to drive at least one of the hooks home, and in consequence the reel line has to be strong; but if all goes well and the hooks are set, then stand by for fireworks as several pounds of extremely concerned fish finds itself restricted and endeavours to rectify the state of affairs.

The other winter fish is the perch, a bristling brigand of the reeds with a mouth like a satchel and an appetite to match. In recent times perch suffered from a mystery disease which decimated their numbers and they became a rare catch in any fisherman's bag. But fortune has smiled again on old stripey and large shoals of both small and medium-sized perch are appearing in their old haunts.

Perch with spinner

Water vole

Like pike, perch will take a spinner; this is a contraption with a single or treble hook fitted to the rear of a spoon-shaped piece of metal. Spinning is a popular way of catching fish, for it takes the angler on a tour of the water and allows him to appreciate to the full the beauty of the countryside. To walk the bank, casting into likely pools and then retrieving to give the metal spinner life enough to fool the fish; to experience the flood of adrenalin which courses through the veins as the fish takes with a thump; to feel the buck and jar of the light rod transmitting the power of the fins against the water, as the fish dashes for some snag or hollow; to enjoy the triumph when, after the struggle is over, the fish, slabsided and barred with red-tinged fins and spiky dorsal fan, is drawn over the edge of the net: this is fine sport for a cold winter's day.

Fishing is more than just catching fish. There is the pleasure of life at the water's edge, from the tiniest crustacean to the shyest dabchick who dives at the approach of the fisher to surface seconds later, with only its head above water, surveying the potential hazard.

In the frost-rimed grass at the water's edge a blunt-nosed water vole sits and chews contemplatively on a crisp stem of watercress held delicately in its five-fingered paws, at ease yet ready to pop into the water and dart under the surface like a stream of quicksilver should danger threaten. When the ice closes over the water the vole can forage underneath for food, safe from the airborne predators. Only the patient pike, poised on barely moving fins, poses a threat to this furry aquanaut.

5

FEBRUARY

February! The month when all of nature seems to be in limbo, halfway between the snows of winter and the warm rain of the coming spring. A time when new lambs stand shivering beside their warm-fleeced dams. 'February fill-dyke' is the term applied to this month by the East Anglian fenmen, though the fens themselves are now only a memory recorded in the legends of 'Hereward the Wake'.

Long ago, before the fens were drained, when the cathedral city of Ely was an island, the flood plain of the Wash stretched almost to Bedford and this was a very different place. It was a wetland, wild with the sound of millions of duck and geese, the haunt of bittern and the wide-winged marsh harrier who quartered the gold and grey plumed heads of the reedbed, dropping like a stone on to the coots which flocked in their thousands to the winter refuge of the watery fastness.

'Fen tigers', the hard men of those times, dragged a living from the harsh marshland in winter and endured intolerable attacks from malaria-carrying mosquitos in summer; nevertheless they harvested the wildfowl and the fish of the fens with incredible fortitude. Strangely, they did not welcome the draining of their inhospitable land by the Dutch and fought each new dyke with a ferocity which the gentry of those times could not comprehend.

When at last the fens were drained and the mosquitos eradicated, the ducks no longer flocked to the wild reedbeds in their millions and the marsh harrier was reduced to a relic few. The human population could no longer eke out a living from the eel traps or the reedbeds so they began to farm the rich black peaty soil uncovered from beneath the dead reeds. It is said that you can plant a walking stick in the soil of the fens and it will grow. This richness is the result of 150,000 years of peat having been laid down from generations of reeds which flourished after the retreat of the ice at the end of the Pleistocene era. But more research needs to be done on how to farm peatland more effectively. Now the fenland and its peat are being blown away, because the mummified plant remains oxidise on contact with the dry fenland winds – so much so that roads built at the time of the draining of the fens now stand 10 ft above the fields with which they were level 100 years ago.

Peat is a valuable commodity for both gardening and farming, but in some places it has become so depleted that ploughs are turning up the buttery clay which forms the bed of the original prehistoric shallow lakes; and everywhere peat lands are being eroded. Even the peat of the Somerset levels in the West Country is being harvested by machines. This is rather sad because although peat is useful as a growing medium it also gives us a unique glimpse into the past. The conditions necessary for the formation of peat are acidity and lack of oxygen. These preserve plant remains almost perfectly, providing a record of climate and herbage over hundreds of thousands of years. A peat bog provides excellent conditions for preserving animal remains as well. The men of the Tollund Bog in Denmark were preserved in this way and they are as perfect as if they had died recently. The chances of finding a similar set of human or animal remains in the Somerset peat deposits are remote, as the commercial exploitation of peat there produces a granulated product in which any remains would be too small to be recognisable.

One feature of fenland farming is the discovery, by ploughing, of perfectly preserved tree trunks. These hindrances to the plough are called, collectively, bog oaks, although some are of other species. The wood is very hard and still usable and has appeared in various guises, but as with all semi-fossilised organic material bog oak tends to oxidise on contact with the air. The fate of most trees uncovered by the fenland plough is to be burned at the side of the field.

It is not only the historical record which is being destroyed with the peat; draining the fens resulted in the loss of one of the most vivid of

Large copper butterfly (*Lycaena dispar batavus*), introduced to Woodwalton Fen from Holland in 1915

the British butterflies, the copper *(Lycaena dispar)*. This beautiful butterfly was dependent on the great water dock plant and the general fenland environment. When these disappeared, before the end of the last century, so did the butterflies. All that remains to remind us of these special creatures are a few dead specimens in collections.

A group of entomological enthusiasts and scientists have attempted to reintroduce a Dutch sub-species of this insect *(Lycaena dispar batavus)* to an area of suitable habitat at Wood Walton fen in Hunting-donshire. It is almost identical to the extinct British insect except that the markings on the lower side of the wing are slightly different. It is breeding, albeit slowly, but because of lack of suitable habitat it will be limited to Wood Walton and perhaps one or two similar fens. Perhaps it is time for us to look carefully at any proposed violent change in our surroundings for although extinction is part of evolution, we do not have the right to pre-empt nature's plan by speeding up the process.

As February wears on there is a quickening in the pulse of the countryside and in the Lake District ravens croak and spiral over the loose scree of the high tops, showing off their aerobatic prowess to their prospective mates, who will soon be sitting in their bulky untidy nests in the tops of hanging oaks on the fellside.

In south-east England male kestrels flutter love signals to their brown falcons. The males, which are smaller with slate-blue heads, show off by performing spectacular stoops, diving from a great height and swooping past the falcon, who utters her high-pitched contact call and spirals up to meet her lover. Legend has it that birds are betrothed on 14 February, St Valentine's Day, and for the kestrel this appears to be more or less true, but for the bird world in general, just finding enough food to stay alive is the uppermost thought in their minds.

February, like January, is a bird table month. Yet the habit of feeding scraps and peanuts to wild birds has only become widespread over the last few decades, a fact which probably can be linked to the overall increase in human prosperity. Forty or fifty years ago erecting a flat board on the top of a pole to provide a dining area for birds would have been considered decidedly eccentric, but now there has grown up around the garden bird table a multi-million-pound industry, supplying the tables themselves, metal or plastic peanut holders, the peanuts to fill them, seed hoppers, wild-bird seed mixtures and so on. Strange edifices indeed are erected in suburban gardens. But in fact the awakening of interest in birds and wild creatures has been the salvation of many garden species. The lack of suitable habitat inherent in a town, and the amount of disturbance created by people, cars, pussy-cats and so on, would otherwise limit the wild bird population to the most hardy and adaptable species, such as the robin, blue tit, blackbird and chaffinch, all of which can be seen from Land's End to John O'Groats.

A direct consequence of birds' co-existence with man has been the increase of one bird in particular, the chaffinch. Not so long ago the chaffinch was in decline. Usually known as a farmyard bird, it lived mainly on left-over grain from horse feed, and with the demise of the horse as the motive power on the land its numbers decreased. The use of dieldrin and aldrin seed dressings almost finished it off completely; the chaffinch became very rare until winter feeding in suburban gardens started it back on the road to recovery.

Our motorised society has now picked up the threads again of our long-lost love affair with the horse and hundreds of free-handed pony

Chaffinch

owners leave grain scattered about. The species' success is now assured, even the dreadful winters of the early 1960s did not affect its progress too badly, whereas these winters dealt a disastrous blow to the wren and long-tailed tit populations.

Bird tables erected in a rural area where the habitat is more varied can attract unusual visitors, such as the lesser and greater spotted woodpeckers, the jay and the nuthatch. Not only do they help our birds directly, but also indirectly, for the public at large have become more aware of the countryside, of the interest of watching birds, and more vocal about habitat destruction and pollution. Modern technology generally has begun to give people more time to worry about the quality of life.

My nomadic family came to rest, temporarily, in the north Cornish seaside town of Newquay when I was nine or ten. The contrast between the rolling hills and deep wooded valleys of north Devon and the wild Cornish coastline with its winter gales, bringing waves crashing house-high on to the golden deserted beaches, was a revelation to me, for although I had been to the seaside many times the stern granite cliffs were unlike any I had seen before.

The birds which inhabited the cliffs were different too. These were guillemots and razorbills, small penguin-like creatures winging in to nest on the inaccessible crags of the headland, croaking and grunting on their white-washed ledges. Back then, in the 1940s, before the summer holiday trade changed the habitat, I was able to wander alone along miles of golden sand never seeing another soul or even a footprint. The wildlife was there if you cared to look and seals with faces like soulful labrador puppies would only flop clumsily down the beach to the sea if approached too close, where they would hang in the breakers and watch from a mere 20 ft or so. It was from Tolcarn beach that I saw my first whale. Because of the depth of water, sea creatures would venture inside the bay and disport themselves. Dolphins were frequent visitors and could often be seen playing in the outer swell of the Atlantic rollers.

This particular day it was quite calm, a rare occurrence during winter, and as I looked out over the water I could see great humps appearing and disappearing. My first thought was of mines – in those days it was not unusual to see the long black cylinders of deep-water mines or depth charges on the beach after a gale. But these black shapes were not menacing. As they came closer I could hear the sound of breathing, and it soon became apparent that it was a school of pilot whales, the largest of which must have been close on 30 ft long.

Pilot whale

As they approached the beach their high domed heads and black shiny skins appeared out of the water like large hummocks. There were ten of them, gliding through the water and they came very close to the shore. The beach at Tolcarn shelves deeply and they obviously felt confident enough to venture to the very edge of the beach swell, only 100 yards or so from the beach itself. The whales were snorting gently and gentleness was the overall impression they gave. In spite of their size at no time was their presence threatening and, enthralled, I followed their course along the beach until they turned and headed out into the wide Atlantic. In 1911 a school of these creatures tragically stranded themselves in Mounts Bay. Whales will follow their leaders blindly, even to death. Happily, my whales came to no harm, whilst giving me the intense pleasure of their company.

To a child the thrills of the Cornish Atlantic coast are innumerable and I soaked up the sights and sounds like a sponge. Just around the jutting granite bluff of the headland was the secret estuary of the River Gannel. Like so many estuaries in the West Country it was not created by a river, but was a valley drowned when the seas rose as the glaciers melted after the last Ice Age. In consequence there was not the large expanse of mud found on a river-cut estuary, just sandflats torn through by rivulets of water leaving a pattern of tapestry-like threads in the muddy gold of the estuary floor, as the river threaded its way to the sea.

In the winter, sanderling and oyster catchers, turnstone and knot, were to be seen flocking and wreathing like drifts of smoke as they twisted and turned over the flats, and duck and geese were regular visitors to the river mouth. But it was not these things alone which drew me, like a compass needle to a magnet. The Gannel had other attractions. The late winter run of elvers was one, the glass-like baby eels returned to the river every year in countless millions, writhing up the wet surface of the small waterfall in Trenance gardens. I did not know then of the fantastic journey these tiny, seemingly fragile creatures had already undertaken from their spawning grounds in the depths of the Sargasso Sea. I would fill jamjars with their wriggling bodies until the water in the jar resembled living grey marmalade and could not understand, when inspecting the jar next morning, why

Elvers

there were only one or two elvers left. The others had tired of their incarceration and left the jar in the night to continue their migrations. I suspected my elder brother Don of dumping them in the garden during my absence and it was not until much later, when I learned of the migration urge of the eel, that I forgave him.

It was Don who provided the means of reaching another Gannel attraction and kindling an interest in bygones and antiques. He was the proud possessor of an ex-WD rubber dinghy and, unknown to my mother, it was this frail craft which transported us to the opposite bank of the estuary where the black wooden hulk of the 'Treasure Ship', which was what the owner called it, was marooned. The hulk had been a sailing coaster before being brought to end her days in the small inlet. The tarred planking of her hull was bubbled with age and the once-proud masts were now only 6-ft stubs rising from her scrubbed teak decking.

After negotiating the perilous river crossing we would get to the deck and deckhouse via a wooden stepladder, its bottom rungs slippery through frequent immersion in sea water and a growth of fine green weed. The owner of the ship was a retired sea captain, a bachelor I believe – or if he had a wife, we never saw her. From time to time the kindly captain opened his home and its contents to a few visitors, but to us the ship was always open. He would welcome us on board and take us below decks through the shiny wheelhouse to the fairyland which lay below in the dim interior, smelling of spices and rare woods, gleaming with rich mahogany and polished brass. Here was the collection of a lifetime's travel: shields and spears from far-off places and, wonder of wonders, the most fantastic collection of old musical boxes and mechanical music machines. When wound and activated these machines produced martial music or melodies through a variety of tiny instruments. Drumsticks would tap out a rhythm on small drums while minute bugles and flutes took up the refrain, all to the muted whirr and click of the machinery and the flashing revolving drums of polished brass, carrying instructions to the intricate mechanism.

Here were treasures indeed and for a child it was pure heaven. I don't think the captain realised just how fascinating his collection was or how infectious his enthusiasm. The collection was sold after his death, but I hope it was kept together and that somewhere children are still enjoying it. From that moment on I have been a keen, if haphazard, collector of bric-à-brac, almost a magpie, and one of the first items I collected was a pair of field glasses, vintage First World

War, all brass with beautiful lenses. In their day they must have been very good quality, but the leather which once had adorned the body was missing and much of the nickel plate was a delicate shade of green; also their usefulness for field work must have been questionable. Nevertheless they gave me a certain status among my contemporaries, none of whom possessed glasses, and I wore them as a sort of badge which endowed the user with supernatural powers of observation.

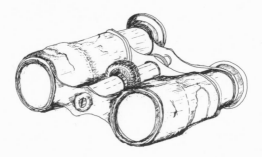

Field glasses

Down by the ponds and streams sluggish movements are becoming apparent. The frogs who have been lying in torpor for the coldest winter months are beginning to rouse themselves from the mud at the bottom of the pond where they have been hibernating and to take off on the pre-nuptial journey back to the pond where they were born.

The males usually reach the water first and sit in the shallows croaking out their rasping love song. Soon after, the females, who are larger, will join them and the males grasp them in a fond embrace with the specially adapted roughened thumbs on their forefeet. They remain coupled thus until 2,000 or so eggs, as small as little black pinheads, are laid, fertilised by the male as they emerge and encapsulated in a thin film of jelly. The jelly absorbs water as it expands and soon becomes buoyant, so the frothy egg-mass floats to the surface of the pond in the familiar form of frogspawn, much beloved of small boys.

The egg-masses are protection for the developing embryo frogs as the sheer quantity confuses potential predators, and also the greatly expanded jelly makes it an awkward mouthful. Laying eggs in February means, too, that there are fewer predators about. The jelly protects the eggs themselves from the cold. Regrettably the 'common frog' is

Frogs and frogspawn, a less frequent sight in the modern countryside

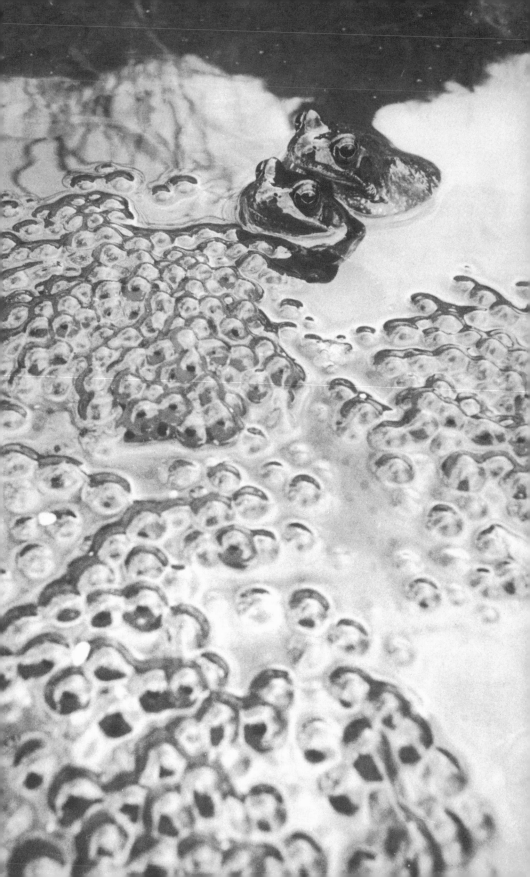

no longer common, for pond and marsh drainage have greatly reduced its homes and spawning grounds. Also the frog is a good subject for teachers of anatomy and biology, and many thousands have been collected for dissection by schools and colleges. As if that were not enough, because they breathe in part through their wet skin, frogs are very susceptible to insecticides. The majority of our frog population lives on farmland for much of the year, so they are right in the chemical firing line.

Not quite so badly affected, but nevertheless decreasing in numbers, is the common toad. This creature makes spectacular migrations during the breeding season to a particular and favoured pool, firmly plodding past all other pools which we casual observers might consider perfect for its purpose. The migration starts as a trickle during February and runs into a flood during March. In one Chiltern village, patrols are organised to guide the toads over a very busy main road they have to cross to reach their pond, and in February and early March people armed with buckets and torches can be seen picking up toads from one side of the road and carrying them to the other side. This slightly eccentric behaviour has certainly saved the lives of thousands of toads which otherwise would have been squashed by unseeing traffic.

Unfortunately, despite such kindly efforts, toads continue to decline, mainly due to loss of habitat, but in some part due to the use of garden pest-control chemicals such as slug pellets, which also kill the toad who eats the affected slug. They are to be encouraged in the garden for they eat a lot of pests. When given the chance they are long lived: ages over thirty years have been recorded for captive animals. Not only do they have a thirty-year effective period, but they are non-pollutant and cost nothing.

Whilst the frogs are disporting themselves in the margins of the pond, the woodland presents a quiet spectacle of inactivity. With the end of the pheasant-shooting season the much-depleted stocks of cock pheasant strut and scratch in the leaf litter, building up their strength for the gladiatorial contests of the coming spring; in the damp places, hidden away deep in the wood, the first thrusting spikes of the primroses bravely push upward into the frigid air. Winter, however, likes to show us she is still in control of the situation and occasionally blankets the woodland floor with another fall of snow. Snow at this time can be particularly difficult for wildlife; the covering of the small remaining food supplies often leads to starvation for the small birds, many of which may be having their first experience of snow. Wrens,

Rook

for instance, may only live for two years or so and do not have time to learn by experience and example how to cope with snowy conditions.

In fact the wren, the treecreeper and other insect-eating birds who find their food on the bark of trees and in crevices have a slightly better time of it than the birds of the open fields. Rooks, especially, are victims of cold weather. The frost renders the ground far too hard for them to pickaxe the plough for worms and grubs which form the mainstay of their diet; and unlike the majority of the corvid clan, crows, ravens and the ubiquitous magpie, the rook does not normally scavenge for carrion. That is not to say it would pass up a free meal if the opportunity was presented, but it tends to stick to its farmland habitat and in hard weather many thousands perish.

However, with the characteristic adaptability of the crow family, rooks have benefited from one of the least lovely manifestations of modern man, the motorway. On nearly every mile of these often featureless roads the metal crash barriers and fences have become perching places for families of opportunist rooks who sit and wait, like undertakers, for flying or creeping creatures to collide with the passing cars. The strategy must be effective for the rooks look healthy enough, even if they are taking into their bodies more lead than their country cousins.

The February snow also brings movements of whooper and Bewick swans. Some of them plane in to land on the Thames and other London waters, where they survey their surroundings in company with our resident mute swans, who stay with us for the summer and breed. Unlike the aptly named mute swan, the whooper and Bewick, who breed on the tundra of Siberia, are extremely vocal. The whooper

Bewick swans

especially has a clanging voice which echoes over the Thames estuary, and the whitefront geese who are also gathering together now fill the air with their wild song, reminiscent of a pack of hounds in full cry.

The cleaning up of the River Thames of the worst of its polluting sewage has allowed the plant growth on the salt marshes of Kent to return to a good enough condition to support a collection of water-fowl which rivals any on the continent. The Thames is a success story in terms of public awareness of pollution in a river system, control of that pollution and reversal of its effects. Twenty years ago the Thames at Chiswick, which was still a fishing community at the beginning of the last century, was to all intents and purposes dead, the only life on the glutinous mud banks which were exposed at low tide being the tubifex worm, a creature of pollution. So many tubifex inhabited the evil-smelling mud that the surface appeared red and a stone thrown on to the mud caused a spasm as the millions of worms withdrew into their tubes in the slime.

Now, twenty years on, and an equal number of millions of pounds spent cleaning the flow, bright gravel shines through, a healthy plant growth flourishes and the fish are there in profusion. Who knows, we may yet see the first February run of Thames salmon for over a hundred years. If we do, it will be something to be proud of.

The valley through which the Thames flows abounds with wildlife and good habitat, far more so than the residents of this, the most overcrowded part of our country, would imagine. The less timid creatures, and therefore the more obvious, such as birds and grey squirrels, can easily be seen in parks and gardens, but even the more unusual and certainly less urban creatures can be found just outside the towns, in the parkland which has been left, like so many green oases, in the sprawl of housing. The history of these 'green lungs' dates back only to the mid-1920s, when the urge to live outside the dirty smoky city centres came upon the middle classes. As the houses spread out on to the farmland and parkland of country houses, the displaced wildlife was concentrated into smaller areas of public open spaces and in consequence these hold a disproportionately high population of wild creatures.

Where this land was untended and scrub allowed to grow, larger wild animals thrived in a strange environment, often undetected by their human neighbours, and gradually, as their numbers increased, they began to move back into the towns by means of the railway – not on the train, of course, but by way of the unpopulated banks along the line.

The steam locomotive with its fire-breathing chimney required the banks beside the railway cuttings to be kept relatively free of vegetation to avoid fires caused by sparks from the train, but with electric and diesel trains over the past ten or fifteen years the banksides have not had to be scalped and sprayed into submission. The increased plant life and the cover it provides allows bigger animals to use the railway banks as a highway, so that now foxes and even badgers can be seen in suburban gardens.

Other creatures have spread into an urban environment too, and several species of deer have become quite common over the past few years without many people noticing. The two prime examples are the muntjac or pig deer and the Chinese water deer, now widespread in the home counties. The little Chinese water deer escaped from the park at Woburn Abbey and has since spread up to the outer fringes of north London. Its success is largely due to the fact that it is very retiring and only about as big as a medium-sized dog. Unlike many other deer it has a large number of fawns, up to six at a time, and although its favourite haunts are in deep undergrowth by the water's edge, it seems to be able to adapt to a wide range of habitat.

The muntjac is larger, almost the size of a labrador dog, and unlike the Chinese water deer the buck has antlers, small spiky tines growing at the back of his head. His defensive armament is supplemented by tusks or sharp teeth which grow from the upper jaw and look like the

91

Muntjac bucks

tusks of a wild pig, bringing the muntjac its secondary name of 'pig deer'. In wooded areas they can be coaxed to overcome their shyness by feeding them apples, which will also tempt them into secluded gardens, having an almost magnetic effect on them.

The bucks have a flap of skin on the cheek which conceals the scent glands they use to mark their territory, rubbing them on a low-growing branch or tree root. In the breeding season, or rut, the buck has a call reminiscent of a fox or small dog.

Although it was first introduced into East Anglia in the early part of the century it has become common over most of the south-east and has even been seen as far west as Bristol and as far north as Manchester. But the muntjac is especially common in the Chilterns and is often flushed by beaters during pheasant shoots, when it bursts away out of covert showing its creamy-white rump patch. Occasionally it is mistaken for a fox, as its coat is rusty-red and the way it runs is not at all like a deer: its hindquarters are higher than the forequarters and in consequence it appears to be running downhill even on level ground.

Although muntjac venison is good to eat these deer are not often killed by man, partly because they do little damage to crops, which may well account for their rapid spread. Young muntjac are sometimes taken by foxes, but they tend to stay with the doe and have few problems from large predators.

6

MARCH

Quite often the wintry February weather continues into the first weeks of March, but there is a different spirit in the countryside. The birds and animals who inhabit the woodlands and hedgerows begin to establish their territories for the coming breeding season and birds who have wintered here become restless for their northern homes. Above the London reservoirs and the grey city, the smew are already flying about rehearsing the nuptial flight they must deploy in earnest when they reach the forests of Russia and Finland.

On hillsides and moorlands, sheep are giving birth to spring lambs and the shepherds' lights burn through the night in the wooden-sided huts. Although the process of sheep-rearing has not changed drastically in the past thousand years, the lot of the shepherd certainly has. In a generation, the lonely man tending his flock on the chalk hills and downlands of the home counties and the Wessex uplands has become merely a memory.

Modern transport and communications have removed the need for a man to watch the flocks day and night and keep tabs on them by listening to the sound of the bells which hung from their necks. It was said by the old shepherds that if a sheep lost its bell it would suffer severe anxiety until a new one was fitted. Now the hills have been enclosed and the sheep no longer wander over wide expanses of country. They graze within the confines of barbed wire and mesh fencing.

Modern veterinary medicine has reduced some of the multitude of ills which afflict sheep, but the lambing season is still fraught with hazards and a man is still needed to tend the ewes in the time of their confinement.

Sheep seem to be stupid creatures and one wonders how they have managed to survive long enough to become a domestic animal. Even the instinct for self-preservation is not very strong in the majority of our domestic breeds, although there are sheep living on the Shetland Islands who are able to fend for themselves, finding nourishment and making good use of it.

Sheep of some breeds have a propensity to fall over onto their backs and then are unable to right themselves. Even the hardiest moorland breeds get themselves into this predicament and have to be helped up by the shepherd with the aid of his crook. How they managed after a heavy fall of snow in places like Dartmoor, the Welsh hills or the Yorkshire Dales before the advent of the tractor or helicopter is a small miracle. Yet we still need sheep – the qualities of wool remain unmatched by synthetic fibres.

The Outer Hebridean islands of Harris and Lewis earned fame, if not fortune, by producing tweed spun on cottage hand-looms from local wool. It is still dyed with natural materials, which give a quality to the finished fabric rivalling the subtle colours of a masterpiece in watercolour. Tweed is forever returning into fashion for no other fabric so well combines the warmth, hard-wearing qualities and weather-resistance traditionally required for country life and its pursuits.

Sheep are also vital to the fabric of the landscape, for they have shaped the land almost as much as man has himself, and a number of insects and plants now depend for survival on the land being grazed by the flocks. Although sheep graze hard they do not destroy the vegetation, and in consequence the normal rank long-growing grasses are suppressed and the more delicate flora, especially of chalk downland, are free to grow and thrive. This is particularly true of the orchid family, who at this time of year, with the frost still on the slopes and only the toughest grasses providing the sheep with a bite, are buried deep in the close mat of grass roots, waiting for the spring sunshine to coax them up into the air to bloom.

Chalk downland shows the influence of sheep more than almost anywhere else. If the sheep are removed the rank grasses will choke all

Dartmoor sheep and lambs – survival specialists in a hostile environment

but the hardiest vegetation, and in time, as has happened on parts of the Chilterns, there is a slow growth of hawthorn scrub, which in turn provides a nursery for hardwood trees such as beech, oak and ash. Before the outbreak of myxomatosis, sheep had help from rabbits in keeping the hillsides open and free from scrub, but with no rabbits and fewer sheep nearly all the tops of the downs are covered with embryo forests.

Even the animal life of the downland is different without sheep. Because of the increased cover the bird life changes; blackbirds sing where once the lark soared up into the air, and ground-living predators like stoats find more cover from which to raid the winter-weakened coveys of grey partridges, lowering the population of this declining bird still further.

Although chalk soil supports a variety of wild plant species, it has in fact a low overall fertility. Each species present on the downland sward is particular to its own niche and will not flourish in another habitat, so despite the profusion of species most of them are interdependent. Unfortunately, the mere act of ploughing chalk downland is enough to break the chain and over the past twenty years agriculture has encroached on the amount of downland available for wildlife.

This is also true of another type of habitat, heathland, again only marginally fertile with a specialised flora and dependent animal population. At the end of the eighteenth century there were large tracts of heath in many of the sandy-soiled parts of Hampshire and Dorset. This land was largely unsuitable for cultivation because of the dryness of the sandy soil, but the Forestry Commission found it ideal for their conifer plantations, and now only pockets of the original heath are left on the edge of the New Forest and in Dorset.

During the drought of 1976 many of the remaining isolated pockets of heathland habitat were devastated by heath fires; the creatures dependent on them were destroyed, having nowhere to run.

Birds such as the hobby, and the secretive insect-eating Dartford warbler whose numbers have dropped to relic proportions, are occupying what remains of the Dorset and south Hampshire heaths. The Dartford warbler does not migrate in winter, but both are at the very northern limit of their breeding range. It is almost inevitable that the warblers will become extinct in our countryside despite the efforts of conservation groups to protect them and their habitat, for the

Dartford warbler

97

number of breeding pairs is just too small to resist the mortality a prolonged cold spell would bring. The Dartford warbler was probably marked for extinction anyway because of its specialisation, but man has speeded up the process.

Among other creatures that have suffered over the past twenty years from the effects of man upon his environment, the otter is outstanding. As a child I was certain to see evidence of otters in the River Thrustle which ran at the bottom of the steep-sided valley near my North Devon home, and these sleek animals would fish for eels in the deep quiet pools formed by the bend of the river. I have watched them too on another Devon river, the Dart, between Buckfastleigh and the moor when fishing for sea trout which run up from the sea in spring and summer.

Otters are creatures who need quiet. If you are able to observe them for any length of time you will notice that they are constantly on the alert, and an unexpected sound will have them diving underwater for cover and swimming away followed by a trail of bubbles.

Over a period of three years I observed a family of otters in a pool in the Dart, a mile or so downstream from the road bridge at Buckfastleigh. Family is perhaps an incorrect description for the dog otter was not usually in residence, but spent his time hunting for eels in the

Otter's holt on the Dart, now sadly unoccupied

Otter with eel

upper part of the river. There does not appear to be any particular breeding season for these animals and young otters can be seen at various times of the year and in various stages of development, from cubs, not much larger than a fully grown stoat and rather doubtful of the rushing water, to youngsters almost as large as their mother.

The reasons this particular pool was so good for otters were its seclusion and a large oak on the bank; its dense root system had been washed clear of soil by frequent flash floods, and the crevices beneath the roots formed a completely secure holt for the bitch otter to bring her cubs into the world. The tree was very old and evidence of wear on the roots and the smoothness of the rock beside the tree suggested that the holt had been used by otters for many years.

In March salmon run up the river, but I never found evidence of the fresh-run fish being taken, although the otters often took the spent, or kelt, fish when they fell back to the sea in the late summer. The usual prey is eels, and the stiff whiskers on the otter's muzzle are perfectly adapted to find these creatures underneath the stones of the river bed. Many a time I sat in a tree overlooking the river watching young otters fishing in this way, turning the stones over with their strong front paws until they found something edible.

Bullheads or loaches also form an important part of the otter's diet and usually these small morsels are eaten underwater, but when they catch eels they always bring them to the bank to eat; they often emerge from the water with an eel gripped in their powerful jaws and its writhing, slimy body wrapped around their necks. This living collar doesn't seem to worry the otters who regard the whole thing as a huge joke and chortle and chatter to themselves whilst unwinding the eel to deal with it.

Humour seems to be a prominent characteristic of otters. They really enjoy life and their capacity for fun and play is tremendous; indeed the slide could have been invented by the otter, for he is a past master at finding one and getting the maximum enjoyment from it. At the head of the pool in the Dart, just where the river flows into it, the bank rises steeply and down the otters used to slide, the earth polished smooth by their lithe wet bodies. One evening I watched them sliding down this slope time after time. They did not always just climb up to the top and slide down head first, although they did this often enough, but also invented variations such as sliding down on their backs with their paws folded across the light fur of their stomachs, all the time chittering with pleasure. Sometimes one of the more inventive members of the family group would stay under water after its slide, emerging with a bullhead or an eel or even a stone in its jaws, which then would be released down the slide with the otter sliding and scrambling after it to try and catch it before the treasure reached the water.

Often the stone or fish would be lost, but this did not seem to matter, as very often the otter would come to the surface with a stone in its mouth when play had started with an eel. There appeared to be little or no hunting attached to the game; it was purely for pleasure. The bitch otter joined in all these games and there was a great display of affection amongst the family, with the cubs nuzzling the bitch and she licking and holding them as a human mother would hold an infant.

Eighteen years or so ago the otters failed to appear at the holt and they have gone from many of their haunts. They were never common, but many rivers held their otter families. The reasons for the decline of these captivating animals seem to be man-made: changes in agricultural practice, land drainage and increased access to the quiet areas of the countryside by a more mobile human population.

The ancient sport of hunting otters must have played a part in their decline, but this was somewhat offset by the valuable role the otter-hunting packs provided in alerting the conservation bodies to the shortage of otters countrywide during the early 1960s, and to do them justice the hunts did discontinue their sport in many areas in an attempt to halt the downward slide.

To help the otters to return to their former haunts we need now to stop 'improving' the river banks. The practice of straightening oxbows, together with the removal of old trees from the waterside, has effectively closed many of the otters' former homes. Increased leisure means increased use of waterways, which poses a future threat to this creature and could prevent its return as effectively as pollution. There is also strong evidence that the use of agricultural pesticides has contributed to otter mortality. As a predator of fish it is at the top of a food chain.

A complication is that trout fishing, once the province of a rich and tiny minority, has become the sport of the masses. Millions of rainbow trout are being raised artificially to stock rivers, streams and lakes which previously held roach, dace and other so-called coarse fish. The trout are raised in stew-pond conditions in a controlled environment and soon lose the instinct of self-preservation. An otter could cause havoc in a trout farm, and the wrath of the owner would be rained down upon its unfortunate head, though it would be doing only what evolution intended. A trout farmer whose livelihood is at stake would understandably pay little heed to the fact that the otter is a protected species under the Protection of Wild Creatures and Wild Plants Act, 1977.

It would help conservation were rate relief to be given to syndicates whose water held otters, and the Protection of Wild Creatures and Wild Plants Act might be amended so that fish farmers and breeders could be reimbursed for adequately protecting their premises against access by predators, thereby avoiding the necessity of killing them. Films like *Ring of Bright Water* and *Tarka the Otter* have stirred public opinion towards the otter, which may bode well for its future.

March is the month when the hares go 'mad', in the southern part of our islands at any rate; in Scotland the crazy-looking courtship ritual is some three weeks later, making it more of an April gambol. In the south the hares are now throwing off their winter blues and racing about showing off their prowess as runners and boxers.

The hare has long been regarded as one of the prime beasts of the chase. It was numbered among the five wild beasts of venery in the Middle Ages, along with hart, hind, boar and wolf. The latter two sadly are no longer with us, exterminated over 200 years ago, but the hare has prospered; as a creature of open country it has suffered less from the grubbing of hedgerows than has most native wildlife. The young leverets are born in the open, and have their eyes open from birth; they can run fast almost as soon as their dense brown fur is dry,

Mad March hares

so open landscape farming suits them literally down to the ground.

Being relatively large animals, hares are vulnerable to shooting and have long been the target of the poacher, which explains why they are missing from certain areas. On the other hand the much-vilified sport of hare coursing has afforded the hare a certain measure of protection on farmland where otherwise it would have been exterminated; as an adult hare can weigh up to 10 lb it can become a pest on farmland, eating large amounts of vegetables and damaging root crops such as turnips and carrots by nibbling them to ground level. Without going into the morality of coursing, it is a fact that where the sport is practised there are more hares than where it is not. However, at this time of year the hares have chasing rather than being chased on their minds, for the jack, as the male is called, resorts to a very special form of territorial display.

The usually solitary hare joins his fellows and indulges in a bout of boxing and horseplay. The does mostly sit and watch, but sometimes they join in the romp and chase the males. The females are nearly always larger than the jack hares and in a boxing match, with both animals standing paw to paw, the doe often subdues her partner.

The hare is an animal which evolution has adapted to evade attacks from predators. Its eyes, large, round and golden-brown, are set high up in its skull and the head is flattened along the plane of the eye so that it can see behind almost as easily as it can see in front. The large pupils are horizontal slits, a useful adaptation to concentrate the vision along a horizontal plane while the animal is running at speed.

Apart from a brief period during March, hares are mainly nocturnal and spend the day resting on open ground in a hollow or 'form', which is occupied for long periods during the year and takes on the shape of the occupant. Their best means of protection in a hostile world is camouflage, and their ability to sit motionless at the base of a tuft of coarse grass until a predator is only feet away, then burst from cover and make off at terrific speed, confuses the potential enemy. Foxes have been seen to run off in fright at a hare erupting from the ground. Unless injured a hare can outrun any of its enemies. Hares can be 'called' in much the same way as some of the predatory animals, such as the stoat and weasel, by sucking air through almost closed lips. The curious hare will approach very close providing you remain hidden.

Brown hares are distributed all over the country, but in the highlands of Scotland and over 1,500 feet above sea level in the northern moorlands of England lives a relic of our last Ice Age – the 'blue' or 'variable' hare. These animals have adapted to live in a cold climate and have retained the ability to change the colour of their fur to white in winter. The blue hare is smaller overall than the brown, with a larger, more rounded head and larger eyes. The two are quite different species, but display much the same breeding pattern. The blue bucks and does meet in the early spring and indulge in the same chasing and boxing performances. The leverets are born from April to early June and are among the most beautiful of all baby creatures, with brindled grey-brown fur and round faces. Mortality of the leverets is heavy: foxes, eagles, buzzards and even crows will attack them, but the doe does not give up easily and will vigorously defend her fluffy young. Their habitats, wild moorland, cannot support a large population of grazing animals and only the fittest survive, which is how nature intended it to be.

The blue hare colonised the British Isles whilst much of the land was still covered in ice from the last Ice Age, which ended 10,000 years ago. It spread north as the ice retreated, living on tundra vegetation for which it is perfectly adapted.

The brown hare followed thousands of years later as the land and the climate warmed, and eventually the blue hare was isolated in the far north where conditions suited it. The blue hare also reached Ireland before the ice melted and the sea rose, but the brown hare must have missed the last ice floe from Liverpool; there are no brown hares in Ireland and the blue hare has adapted to fill the niches which the other species occupies on the mainland.

The last Ice Age shaped the landscape which produced the flora and fauna of the British Isles as we know it today. When the ice retreated it left behind a sterile landscape; not even worms were able to survive the

Fossil strata in the cliffs along part of the Dorset coast, where the pages of the book of time are open; Charmouth and nearby Lyme Regis saw the birth of scientific study of the age of dinosaurs

Crushed ammonite found in the Charmouth ammonite beds. These creatures had squid-like bodies protected by a pearly shell; they swam in their millions in the shallow warm sea which lapped the Dorset shores when mighty lizards were kings of the prehistoric world

intense cold which shattered the toughest rock. The glaciers created a scraping effect as they moved slowly over the land. They carried with them the collected soil, rocks and gravel from other parts of the country, re-depositing them in valleys as the ice sheet melted. The immense pressure of thousands of millions of tons of frozen water rounded off the sharp edges. Only the hardest granite surface was able to withstand the forces at work. Subsequently central England, which is mainly composed of softer sedimentary rock, took on a rolling aspect and the slowly retreating ice left behind a rich fine soil all ready for recolonisation by plants from the warmer south, and the animals, insects and birds dependent upon them.

This process of recolonisation was temporarily halted by the melt-water flooding the vast basin which is now the North Sea and also the flooding of the chalk valleys which became the English Channel. In consequence of the (relatively recent) formation of Britain as an island we do not share with the continent of Europe some of the creatures who were latecomers from the south. Only the birds have continued the process of recolonisation with their winter and summer migrations.

What a fascinating spectacle the thawing landscape must have revealed. As the land warmed and the seas rose and advanced further inland, flooding estuary valleys in the southern part of England and Wales, the country must have presented an aspect of ever-changing spring. As the climate grew milder and the land dried out, the mosses, which were the first plants to cover the naked earth, quickly gave way to flowering plants and then by degrees to birch scrub and finally flower-covered downland and rich forests. Man had yet to make his presence felt, for he numbered merely a few thousand over the whole country. The landscape was far from the desolate wilderness often depicted and our forefathers lived in a colourful world of birds, insects and animals and above all with a carpet of flowers. It was a land of plenty, and the cave dwellings were not dark and dank or forbidding. Ancient man lived in the British equivalent of the Garden of Eden.

Pussy willow

As the month of March progresses we see the re-enactment of a series of events which happened all those thousands of years ago and has been continuing ever since. The lengthening of the days brings the promise of spring and in the cold earth there are stirrings of life. The dog's mercury presses its green leaf-fronds up through the litter on the woodland floor and primroses carpet the rides and clearings. Pussywillow catkins and hazel 'lamb's tails' dust pollen on the wind to fertilise the fruit. In the meadow, the first daisies open shy eyes to the

Speedwell

warming sun and the speedwell shines blue from the tangle of last year's brown undergrowth.

An air of excitement pervades the countryside; the town robins sing and posture on the garden fence proclaiming their territory for all to hear; the wistful notes are gone and the new song has all the challenge of a Sousa march. In town gardens, where the heat from buildings bestows a micro-climate two or three degrees above the surrounding countryside, the song thrushes are starting to build their sugar-bowl nests and sing from the television aerials in the evening.

Along the roadside verges bright yellow coltsfoot makes its presence felt, the dandelion-shaped and coloured flower heads thrusting up into the air on scaled stems. Coltsfoot was awaited with genuine concern by country people of old, for it was from this plant that a remedy was compounded for long-lasting winter coughs; it was a favourite herb with ancient apothecaries who often used it for infections of the lungs. Other weapons in the herbal armoury included shepherd's purse which was considered beneficial in stopping haemorrhage. All the herbs used for medicinal purposes do contain substances which would alleviate certain disorders; some had more effect than others, but they did work. Some of the chemicals used in modern drugs are to be found in our wild plants. Willow bark, for instance, was used even in my own childhood as a pain-killer: it contains an acid which has been synthesised and named 'aspirin'.

Not all herbs were used as medicines. A great many of them found their way into the kitchen to flavour the food and others had more specialised roles. The leaves of the butterburr, which is pushing its heavy head through the litter just now, were used to wrap round butter; but these are yet to come. Only the bulbous pink flower-head is showing above the soggy ground at the ditch side. Above the ditch the blackthorn buds are starting to burst, decking the hedge with a dusting of blossom to which the early insects will fly for a sip of nectar, the first of the flood of sweetness the coming year holds. In the woodlands of the West Country, above the celandines, buzzards mew and call to one another and weave sticks together in the fork of ancient oaks, forming a wheelbarrow-full of branches into an untidy nest for their eggs.

This month heralds the beginning of the greatest movement of living creatures on earth, the annual migration of countless millions of birds from the Horn of Africa to their northern breeding sites. The

Sweet violet

108

swallows and martins are gathering in large flocks prior to their departure for the meadows of England. It will be four or five weeks before the vanguard reaches the south coast, but the scene is set.

In the cities the vast throng of squeaking starlings who crossed the North Sea in December to stay for the winter are preparing to return across those hostile grey waters to the continent to whistle the songs of a London winter in the streets of Hamburg and Copenhagen. The northern redwings and the fieldfares are on their way to the birch and pine forests of Scandinavia, but in Scotland a few will stay to set up territories and nest. The wild moors of the Scottish lowlands ring with cries of the curlew as they stake their claims among the heather, while the grouse call 'go back, go back' from gullies in the fellsides and glens, where the snow is still lying in patches like heaps of granulated sugar.

As the month wanes, in the softer climate of southern England the woodland margins are beginning to bloom. Sweet violets peep shyly from the shade and pinkish-blue wood violets raise their heads to the

Wild daffodil

pale sunshine which slants through the wood. In the rides the wild daffodils brandish their spears to the warming winds; the plants of the March woodlands and meadows can cope with the temporary chill, for the wind, although cold, has not the desiccating dryness of February. Frost is still a problem to plants, though, and the first of the sheltered woodland species to raise their vulnerable flowers, risking the next generation of their kind, do so in order to get ahead in the seed-production cycle before the more vigorous plants of late spring develop in a welter of showy blooms, confusing the pollinating insects.

In the confines of the ponds the toads are taking over where the frogs have left off, and below and in between the masses of jelly left by the frogs, stretch the twin lines of black-dotted toad spawn. The strengthening sun's rays have warmed the bundles of life, the tadpoles are developing and there is a hint of movement in the mass of forming cells.

Below the frogspawn, in the ooze at the bottom of the pond, lurk the predators. Dragonfly larvae with their hinged and prehensile mouthparts await the rain of tadpoles like gatecrashers at a feast. Life down there too is beginning to move. It is fortunate for the pond dwellers that water becomes denser as its temperature drops. When the temperature reaches between 0° and 3°C it reverses the process, and in consequence of this interesting phenomenon ice forms on the surface but not at the bottom of a pond. To the denizens of both mud and water this is more than an interesting fact – it is a matter of life and death.

Because the water at the bottom of a pond remains at 3°C during freezing weather the pond life can continue to swim and breathe in liquid water; in fact breathing becomes easier as very cold water has more dissolved oxygen in it. This is probably why insects and other water creatures can remain relatively active during extreme cold – they have to expend less energy absorbing oxygen. But plankton are almost absent in freezing water, not because of the cold, which they do not seem to mind, but because the available sunlight is too little to enable them to multiply. A pond or small lake is clear in late winter or early spring – there are few creatures in the water to make it cloudy.

Despite the freely available dissolved oxygen, the larger occupants of the water, fish like tench or carp, sleep the winter through in the soft enclosing mud at the bottom of the pond. Carp especially can stand being frozen without suffering permanent harm and it appears they have a substance in their bloodstream which acts like anti-freeze, preventing their cell walls being ruptured by the formation of ice crystals in their bodies. In our relatively temperate climate they do not often need to use this facility, but it will be a few weeks before the carp and tench feel the urge to rise from their muddy coverlet and join in the life of the pond, unlike their brethren in the rivers and the larger waters who have only slowed their life processes, not gone into a prolonged slumber.

In the clear water above the mud, daphnia and cyclops dance, forerunners of the millions of their kind who will turn the margins red with the colour of their bodies early in the summer to come. The water plants, crowfoot and watercress, send up buds from the dormant root system, grasping the available light with their spreading leaves, waiting for the time when the sun will strike deep into the water long enough and strongly enough to enable them to grow to their full 'water forest' proportions.

Daphnia and cyclops

On the surface of the mud the caddis-fly larvae creep around carrying their homes on their backs, pieces of stick and dead weed stems which they cement together in a tube to protect their delicate bodies. It will be many months yet before they can make their journey to the surface to become the lacy-winged adult flies so beloved of the trout.

The fishers of trout, the human ones, are looking forward to the end of March, the end of their long winter vigil. Now their thoughts are of nymph and lures and the confections of feathers which the eager rainbows take with a thump. There is just time to sit with a fly vice and

111

concoct from feathers and floss some new flies which, hopefully, will be the flies to end all flies, the ultimate. Although there is no one fly which will tempt all trout to rise there is always hope – as the displays in tackle shops demonstrate. It is a truism among tackle dealers that flies are designed to catch anglers rather than the wily trout. There is no intentional deception, it is just that on being confronted by a display of beautifully tied upwinged 'olives' or 'blue duns', like fairies in silk, the bewildered angler succumbs to temptation every time.

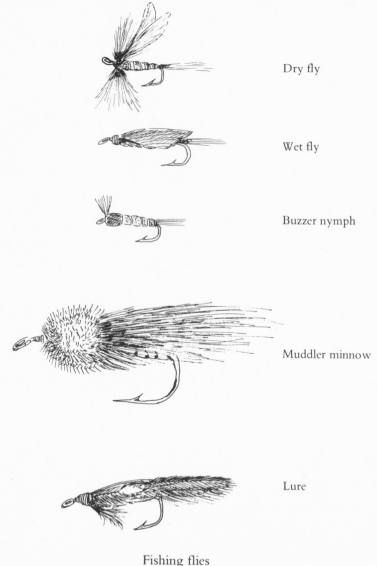

Dry fly

Wet fly

Buzzer nymph

Muddler minnow

Lure

Fishing flies

Take a look at the fly box of the average fly fisher, if such an animal exists; it is a revelation, a multi-coloured display, dazzling like a jewel-box, a fly for all seasons. Closer examination will reveal most of the flies to be new and unused and likely to remain so, as many trout fishers use, at most, only ten fly patterns during the entire season, and indeed their technique is evolved to this end.

There are lure fishers who would laugh at a dry fly and there are nymph fishers who would never dream of using a lure. As in all sports which demand a certain measure of skill there is a type of snobbery. This snobbery used to be confined to those fishermen who aimed to catch trout by presenting a fly on to the water, upstream of the angler, where it would float like a real insect on the surface film over the fish. As an exercise in the skill of accurate casting this method has few equals, but certain fishers started to say it was unethical to catch fish by any other means – which is ludicrous. Many of the largest fish taken from our waters have been taken on lures, large dressings akin to salmon flies in their size and gaudiness. These lures and their presentation demand a different but nevertheless special kind of skill.

Personally I have the greatest difficulty in catching anything on a lure except the bushes behind, and when the lure is in the water it is hard to believe that it will attract a fish. I use nymphs, which are artificial flies tied to resemble insects in their underwater larval stage. With these I have a certain measure of success, probably because I believe in their efficacy and therefore persist with them until an obliging trout comes to the offering. This happens reasonably frequently so I have become addicted to fishing nymphs despite advice to the contrary from well-meaning fishing companions.

The aid more valuable to the pursuit of trout than any other is, simply the human eye – preferably open and looking towards the water, observing the conditions and the way the trout are feeding, and on what they are feeding. This will repay the angler far more than hours of 'chuck and chance' fishing which can disturb the fish, putting them down.

Observation is a must, as there is little value in fishing the surface film when there are no fish showing. Ten minutes reading the water and the life at the water margin will tell the angler volumes; for instance, the empty cases of hatched flies will give an indication of which type of fly to use.

But it is not quite the first of April and trout fishermen must be patient and walk by the water and lovingly tend their tackle and practise casting on the lawn, much to the enjoyment of the cat who

113

seems to think that cotton wool on the end of a fly line is put there solely for his benefit.

March weather is infamous for its changeability and bright days can suddenly be transformed with raging, howling gales in the space of a tide. The blue sea, sparkling in the morning, can become a sullen grey wolf flying at the rocks and breakwaters as though to smash them. This is not so fundamental a problem as it was in the days of sail, when to be caught in a bay with the wind off the sea could be fatal; our coastline is littered with the wrecks of such unfortunate vessels. The March gales of today do not bring ashore the proud four-master; they fling onto our beaches the debris of technology – plastic and oil, and the pathetic corpses of birds caught on the open seas by slicks of slimy crude, discharged by ships washing their tanks.

Oil is the DDT of the sea. It has fundamentally changed the structure of the seabird population in a generation. The puffin, that parrot-billed fisher and clown of the sea who nests on the islands off the Bristol Channel, is now so reduced in numbers that it is in danger of disappearing altogether as a breeding species by the end of the 1980s, largely because of oil. Material wealth, seemingly so vital to modern man, remains totally incompatible with the natural world. As a fellow species surely man has a responsibility for progress without destruction.

7

APRIL

The season's new lambs gambol in the fields and butt, half-grown, on the fresh springing turf. Lapwings 'peewit' in the clear blue of the sky above the newly ploughed brown earth. The first of the shoots can be seen pushing up through the warming farmland, but there is still a risk of frost and the apple trees in the orchards hold their scaly buds closed against the time of blossom.

In the hedge bottom the pollinating bumble bees hum and bumble about, searching out the first nectar-bearing blossoms. This is not the first outing the bee has made; unlike many insects of the bee family, the bumble-bee queen ventures out during the winter cold.

It has been proved, by a computer, that its combination of weight and small wing and muscle area must prevent the humble bumble from leaving the ground; but bees cannot read computer print-outs and happily continue to fly, regardless of the facts. As well as being a flying anachronism, the bumble bee has a mechanism which puts it in a class of its own. It is able to generate enough heat within its body to allow it to maintain a reasonably high level of activity even in very cold weather, and it only needs a few bright days for the queen to take the air. But winter is past now and the buzzing, searching queen is looking for a disused bank-vole's nest in which to found a new dynasty.

The queen is the only survivor from the previous year's colony and she carries in her bulky body the material for a new tribe of workers. The bumble bee is one of nature's great pollinators. Without it the English landscape today would be very different, because many of our wild flowers and most crop plants depend heavily on the efforts of their furry bodies as they crash from flower to flower in the manner of a controlled aerial traffic accident.

There are sixteen members of the genus 'bombus', the family of insects to which the bumble bee belongs, and the first queen to appear in spring is the 'red-tailed bombus pratorum'. A rather small bee by bumble standards this insect makes its home below ground in the nest of some mouse. It is soon joined on its aerial meanderings by the much larger 'bombus terrestris', a large yellow-tailed bee and the one which to most people is the typical bumble bee; its black furry body and yellow-tipped tail is familiar to all. It too is a ground-nesting species.

Bumble bees, unlike honey bees, do not store honey to tide the tribe over the winter; only the queen can withstand the cold months and she

Buttercup with bee

is fertilised before the winter rest. She carries the next generation in her ovaries and when she finds a suitable nest site she begins to build brood cells, ball-shaped structures not at all like the tidy symmetrical shapes constructed by the honey bee. From these brood cells emerge the smaller sterile female worker bees, to found a new colony. Once the workers are hatched and out on their rounds the queen settles down to the serious job of egg-laying and she does not leave the colony again.

The 'bombus' bees have a number of enemies, some of which go to extraordinary lengths to disguise the fact that they are indeed enemies. These are the so-called 'cuckoo' bees, which look very much like their hosts and gain entry to the nest and the brood chamber, substituting their eggs for those of the nest bees. The cuckoo bees have the sense to wait until the host queen has had time to produce sufficient workers to feed the colony and its interlopers.

As well as insect enemies there are larger forms of life who regard the gentle bumble as a meal. Badgers will dig out a nest and eat the brood, and mice are well known for attacking their nests, perhaps a case of natural justice. The famous naturalist Charles Darwin remarked on this to one of his children, when he said that by keeping the mouse population down the family's cats were contributing to the increase of bees in the garden. Man too has played a not inconsiderable part in the decline of the bee and the destruction of hedgerows is a major factor, reducing potential nest sites. This is a strange anomaly when the bumble bee plays such an important part in the fertilisation of food crops.

As the cuckoo bee cannot breed before the bumble bee has a sufficiently large colony of workers to tend its larvae, so the bumbles themselves cannot survive or multiply without the flowers for nectar and pollen, and April is the month when the wild flowers begin to come into their own with the first real flush of primroses on the bankside.

April and the primroses were a part of my childhood and my mother and I would troop off to the hanging oak wood near our house to pick both primroses and sweet violets which grew in profusion, and for weeks afterwards the house would be sweet with their smell. There would also be the delightful sight of yellow celandines and blue periwinkles shining from every pot and jar in the house. One flower, however, was never allowed to cross the threshold – the frothy white sprays of the blackthorn were banned, for like May blossom it was thought to be unlucky. The reason for this superstition has been lost; no doubt there was some pre-Christian significance in the belief that blackthorn brings bad luck. Perhaps also, our ancestors associated the coming of the plague with the time of year when the blackthorn blossoms.

With the lengthening days, the intensity of the sun, rising higher in the midday sky, is calling plants and creatures alike from their winter rest.

Herald of the hoped-for multitude of butterflies, the holly blue, which echoes the colour of the early spring sky in its wings, flits about the hedgerows and woodland margins. This insect produces several generations in a season, through the full development cycle of egg to caterpillar to pupa and perfect insect, during spring and summer and even into the late autumn; but now the males, with their black-tipped wings, are searching for the females, who sit and sun themselves on holly bushes where they will lay the first of this year's generation on the flower buds. The early holly blues do indeed have holly as their food plant, it is only the later generations who will lay their eggs on ivy.

Holly blue

The birds who breed on our shores, but winter in warmer climes, are now starting to arrive back in earnest, and time their arrival to coincide with the hatching of insects that have overwintered as eggs and small larvae. As these grow on the spreading vegetation, one of the first visitors to appear is the smart flycatcher of the oak woodland, the pied flycatcher; it makes its way to ancestral nesting sites in the south-west and the remnants of oakwoods in Wales, moving into the territories which they, or their parents, occupied the previous year. This is one bird whose range has been increased by the hand of man. It is a hole-nesting species and the recent extensive provision of nest-boxes by private individuals and natural history societies has encouraged it to extend its breeding environs. The pied flycatcher tends to be restricted in its normal range to mature woodland which contains the

Pied flycatcher

food it needs and, more important, nesting holes in sufficient quantity to reduce competition from birds like tits and woodpeckers. A sure sign that it has benefited from the additional housing is proved by its northward spread, although it remains a scarce breeding bird in the south-east, as it has been for several hundred years past.

Of all the migrants who visit our shores in the spring perhaps the most familiar is the chiff-chaff – not because it has a showy appearance, but because of its repetitive song. An insignificant, dull greenish-buff warbler, it sings its two-note refrain from the depths of a bush, but despite its retiring habits it is a real harbinger of spring. All over the southern half of England the call can be heard as the male bird proclaims his presence to one and all, and to lady chiff-chaffs in particular. This bird belongs to the sizeable family of hedgerow migrants which includes in its ranks some of the finest songsters we have, birds which make the spring air ring with their mating and territory-warning calls.

The garden warbler is a rich and varied songster. Not for it the boring dual-note song of the chiff-chaff, and it is an active member of the dawn chorus. It may wake later than the resident blackbirds and thrushes and so misses the solo spots taken by the showier, louder-volume birds, but nonetheless without it the early morning symphony would be the poorer.

Chiff-chaff

Migrant warblers make up a large proportion of the garden favourites, some of which are not so common. The blackcap and the
whitethroat are among the band filling the wakening spring with
song, and a characteristic of these birds is their ability to lose themselves in the depths of a bush, only announcing their presence with a
torrent of liquid notes. As a family the warblers are all retiring and
usually of a grey-brown or greenish hue. Apart from the difference in
song there is only a white or yellow eye stripe on the head with which
to identify the different species and so cause ornithologists nightmares
and much recourse to reference books.

Some of the warblers do give the bird watcher, or listener, a clue and
the most easily recognisable of these is the grasshopper warbler, a bird
of the same indistinct smooth shape, but with a song which sounds
just like the continuous well-oiled whirr of an expensive fishing reel,
or an extremely enthusiastic grasshopper or cricket. The sound is
composed of a multitude of varying notes all delivered apparently
without pause for breath. Only by slowing down the bird's song with
a special tape recorder is it possible to detect the separate notes.

The grasshopper warbler has become commoner over the past ten
years, and another member of the family, Savi's warbler, is similarly
colonising reservoirs and gravel pits in the southern part of the
country. Gravel pits are a form of man's exploitation of the countryside which has a positive and decidedly beneficial effect on wildlife.
As the gravel is taken away to create concrete fillers for the building

industry, the holes left by the diggings fill with water. At first they are sterile, but in a relatively short time, and generally with the help of man, the pit margins become clothed with vegetation and the water, where it is reasonably shallow, blooms rich with weed and becomes home to a myriad of forms of water life – including fish, which are often introduced. The scene is then set for a full-scale recolonisation of the area by a varied wildlife.

Grebes, mainly fish-eating great crested grebes, display and grunt their spring song on the surface and coot squabble in the shallows, while the white-sided tufted duck owes its increase as a breeding species almost solely to the provision of the open water afforded by gravel pits. It is not long before the reedy margins chime with the calls of reedwarblers as the reeds begin the process of converting the open water back to dry land. Usually there is a long period, often years, before the gravel workings are again exploited by man, this time for leisure activities such as sailing and fishing, and by this time the wildlife is well established.

The woodcock, a quiet wader of the woody leaf litter of the central belt of England, Scotland and to a lesser extent Wales, is dependent upon a quite different habitat. It is nesting now, laying its grey-white eggs which turn to a rich brown as incubation progresses and the colour of the leaf mould on which the eggs are laid seeps into the shell. Woodcock sit very tight, and usually the first indication of their presence is when a brown, round-winged bird rises from the ground startling you with a guttural croak.

Woodcock

The best time to see woodcock is in the evening during early April when the males patrol the boundaries of their territory. This flight is called 'roding' and the birds give a call which sounds like something between a sneeze and a froglike croak. Woodcock are far commoner than is generally supposed, but they are very secretive, and being largely nocturnal in their feeding habits they are rarely seen except when flushed from their daylight resting places. Cold and frosty weather has a serious effect on their population as their main food is earthworms and when the ground is frozen many woodcock suffer badly. They are popular as a game bird and there is little doubt that the provision of copses and game coverts greatly helps them by providing habitat and feeding areas.

However, the game-shooting season is past and the sound of the beaters through the woods has died away for another year. The blood of other field-sports enthusiasts is coming to the boil, however, for the trout-fishing season is upon us. Rods are taken from their bags and reels are oiled for battle. Fly fishing has an appeal akin to shooting in that the quarry is stalked, seen and aimed for directly. It is a mobile sport, requiring only light tackle and few encumbrances. A wicker creel, the rod, a net and fly box are the only items to be carried, leaving the fisherman free to roam and search for his fish. He finds it rising and casts to it, watching with bated breath as it turns to the fly, seeing the white flash as its mouth engulfs it; then up with the rod top and the fish

Brown trout

is on, diving and shaking, arching the frail rod like a bow as it sounds in the clear water trying to free itself from the restriction of the hook and line: this is the moment when the long months of waiting for the season to begin are forgotten. It is almost an anticlimax when the fish is drawn over the net and lifted from the water. There is a thrill in catching the first fish of a new season which never palls, and whatever its size no other will equal it for adrenalin production.

It is unfortunate that selective breeding has produced trout which attain weights over 6 lb and also a generation of anglers who think that a fish of only 1 lb is a mere tiddler. As a child I was apprenticed to the art of trout fishing by the local constable and in the acid waters of the river Thrustle a trout of half a pound was considered a beauty and one of 1 lb positively a monster. The peat-stained water did contain big fish, but they all ran up from the sea, and in April it was not unusual to see a salmon lying in the deep water which formed the tail of the pool below the bridge on the Tavistock road. These majestic fish, broad tails fanning the stream, were waiting for a spate from the moor to allow them to journey the few remaining miles to the spawning redds.

Like all small boys I could not resist the temptation to try my luck at the salmon, despite a warning from my guide and mentor – who had probably marked that particular fish for himself, planning to visit the pool with a gaff later that same evening. I armed myself with a large worm and a suitable length of braided black and green silk fishing line, the only type available in those days of shortages. From the bridge parapet I carefully lowered the hook with its wriggling captive and watched as it slowly sank into the tea-coloured water. It was taken by a trout of about half a pound before it had sunk even three inches below the surface, and I hauled it up with disgust. It would make good eating as would its three brothers, all of whom ignored the fact that the worm they so eagerly took was intended for their more illustrious cousin. Never before or since have I caught trout with such ease from this stream, but they were not the quarry I had set my sights on. Finally the worm floated down to the bottom without being taken by a trout, although some 'fingerling' attacked it as it bumped tantalisingly over the round stones of the river bed. The salmon ignored it as it trotted past on the weak current, still pursued by small trout for which it was too mighty a mouthful.

Sick with disappointment at my failure I drew in the line intending to have another try. Whether it was the flashing bodies of the small trout attacking the worm which attracted the salmon's attention, or

Child at Salmon Pool Bridge

Salmon spinning on the Dart

whether it was the movement of the worm itself I know not, but the salmon surged forward, scattering the fry, snapped up the worm in a cavernous mouth and swung back to its resting place at the tail of the pool. My ecstasy knew no bounds: I had it. Now it only had to be dragged in. Such is the confidence of childhood! As the fish came to rest on the stones, and before it rejected the worm, I heaved on the line, setting the small trout hook in the salmon's jaw. The king of the river did not appreciate this treatment and showed his annoyance by rushing across the pool like an express train.

I had no reel, nor even a rod, and the line was wound around my fingers, so this action tightened the line until it cut into my skin painfully, but I had no intention of letting it go. The struggles of the salmon became more determined and the line around my fingers drew tighter; with a rush it took off rapidly upstream, thrashing over the shallows below the bridge and out into the pool on the other side. At this point the line, which mercifully for my hand was weakened, probably by age and long storage, parted and I was left with tears of pain and frustration in my eyes, the agony of squashed fingers overshadowed by the disappointment at losing the salmon. On its side, 'Salmo the leaper', monarch of migratory fish, had been in little danger from my amateur efforts to wrest it from its natural element, and the small trout hook and short piece of line would have caused little trouble. It would have been shed from the skin around the jaw within a few days, leaving only a small white scar.

The loss of that fish damaged my ego considerably. Even though the fact that I had hooked it at all was a happy accident and its loss a foregone conclusion, in my mind it had lain on the bank and was mine, my first salmon. The actual reality of a first salmon on the bank was not to come for fourteen years, on the bank of another Devon river, the Dart.

Away from the river bank the thin and hungry hedgehog is wakening from its winter sleep and snuffling the hedge-bottoms with an urgency born of desperation. After the dormancy of the past months it is dangerously low on fat under its spiky hide and is vulnerable to the sudden sharp frosts which often occur at this time of year. Although prickles can withstand the cold when in deep hibernation, once awoken his metabolism is quite high and he needs all the food his questing nose can find. Hedgehogs will not breed until the layer of fat on their bodies has been built up enough and the mother hedgehog can capture enough food for her developing young.

This food can be quite varied, for the hedgehog will eat almost anything from insects to plants or carrion, and performs a very useful task in demolishing creatures which farmers and gardeners regard as pests. If you have a hedgehog in the garden you will not need to use slug pellets or any kind of slug bait.

All over the countryside vixens are nuzzling their tiny blind squeaking cubs, for early spring, and April especially, is the time when the litter of two or three young is born. Foxes make superb mothers and will go to extraordinary lengths to protect the earth and disguise it. In fact foxes who have earths in the suburbs of some of our major towns often go undetected until unwary cubs venture out on inquisitive missions into flower beds and such like.

Another even more secretive animal, the badger, has had her cubs for a month or so and they are beginning to make their presence felt in the close confines of the sett. But it is not until the early weeks of May that they will squint myopically at the outside world from the safety of the sett entrance, and only then if the sow badger has made sure that the coast is truly clear.

As the early purple orchid opens to the spring sun, the pheasants in

Early purple orchid

the coverts will have completed their showy mating ritual, when the cocks stamp and strut in front of the seemingly unresponsive hens, and now those hens are sitting above their slowly increasing clutch of putty-coloured eggs. Out in the meadows, male grey partridge are running to and fro in front of the females inciting them to courtship and mating, and in the centre of the field lapwings are performing their aerobatics in the clear air.

Chittering with frustration at a meal so near and yet so far overhead, the stoat stands at the entrance to its burrow, a home stolen from a rabbit or a rat which provided a meal for this hedgerow tiger. But she will not move far from the burrow, for deep underground is her litter of five kitts, blind and helpless and covered in white fur. The stoat is a tender mother; although a fearless hunter she is the most caring of all the weasel clan. In the south of England the stoat does not change its coat for the royal ermine which distinguishes its northern relatives. None the less the ability to do so lies there in the animal's gene pattern and the stoats of the south can, under exceptional weather conditions, grow a white coat. Ermine, as the white winter pelage is known in the fur trade, was much prized as a trimming for garments, especially for robes of state, but the conservation lobby has had its way and their Lordships in the House of Lords now have their robes trimmed with an artificial substitute, much to the relief of the Scottish stoat population.

The timing of the birth of predatory animals is logical, coinciding with the flush of new life amongst their prey. This is the usual pattern in the wild. Birds such as the sparrowhawk will establish a territory and occupy a disused nest, possibly that of a carrion crow, but the female will not hatch her young until there is an ample supply of easily caught prey in the shape of young songbirds and chaffinches, to form the bulk of the diet for the downy chicks. So too with the majestic buzzard, the eagle of the south-west hillsides and woodland. The two chicks of the buzzard brood are fed almost exclusively on young rabbits and voles, an easily caught prey.

Birds of prey are especially vulnerable to the effects of man upon the environment; witness the decline of all species following the introduction of DDT, organochlorine and organophosphorous compounds to control insect pests on the land. It is only over the last few years that some of these predators have begun to increase again. Peregrine falcons are one of this group. They declined almost to extinction, but they appear to be slowly returning to their old haunts. Habitat destruction was not the problem for this fine creature; when it comes

Buzzard

to nest sites the falcons usually choose wild and inaccessible territory. Their main threat now comes from a band of unscrupulous individuals who resort to the practice of nest-robbing in order to satisfy the desire of some falconers to possess a peregrine, the ultimate in hunting birds.

Falconry has its roots deep in the tradition of our past history, when the peregrine was the falcon of kings and nobles and other ranks in society had to hunt with the smaller falcons or hawks. However, times have changed and there is now, regrettably, a good case for controlling the practice of falconry, in the interest of the bird. There is something thrilling about the co-operation of man and a bird in free flight and it would be a pity if the skill of the falconer was lost. How much better, though, to see a wild falcon stooping down the wind at its prey. Even the less spectacular birds of prey, the kestrel and the sparrowhawk, are captured both as nestlings and adults for this sport, and because they need expert handling for their wellbeing they frequently die in captivity.

As with garden birds, predatory birds can be encouraged to nest, in areas where they are scarce, by providing nest boxes and platforms in trees in secluded woods and coppices. Sparrowhawks take over the homes of crows or rooks, but an imitation on a platform may persuade one to nest. A nest box for a kestrel needs to be about the size of an apple box, and some success has been obtained by nailing half a barrel to a tree and partially boarding the open end. Boxes or barrels of this type will also serve for tawny owls, and the much depleted barn owl may well breed successfully if a box is fixed in the roof of a new farm building.

But all this could count for nothing unless gamekeepers and farmers allow birds of prey on their land. This is not such an unreasonable demand as it appears, for birds of prey tend not to make game birds a major part of their diet, and the few birds they do take are the weaker ones which the keeper would be better without, the end result being a healthier overall stock.

Head of sparrowhawk

Birds of prey regurgitate the hard, horny, bony parts of their food that they cannot digest, and analysis of these pellets reveals what they eat. For instance, examination of the pellets of the sparrowhawk, a bird much persecuted by keepers in the past and, despite the protection offered to it by legislation, still killed on some of the less enlightened estates, has shown game birds to be almost absent from the prey it catches. High on the food list, though, were wood pigeons, definitely not friends to either farmer or gamekeeper. Observation has shown that a patrolling pair of sparrowhawks will keep a field free of feeding 'woodies' more effectively than shooters in bale hides or gas guns and scarers.

Stickleback

Modern game management does not rely on the outdoor rearing of pheasants and other game birds so at the time when the young would be most at risk they are safe in their enclosures. Weather, and disease that sometimes accompanies intensive rearing, are nowadays greater threats to them than predators.

As April progresses the countryside pulses, the sun reaching ever higher, adding life-giving heat to the melting pot of nature. Male sticklebacks, resplendent in their coats of shiny red and green, joust like tiny knights amongst the pond weed, vying for the affections of the drab females, luring them down to the dark recesses of the nests built for them. The female's reluctance to enter the cosy nest is hard to understand, for having ejected the eggs from her distended abdomen her part in the saga of rearing new life will end. After he has fertilised the eggs in the nest the male will lavish paternal care upon them, fanning fresh water over them with his fins, turning and tending the growing embryos, defending them against all comers until they hatch, while the female swims away to enjoy herself in the warming water of the pond.

Above the crinkled mirror surface of the water where the gnats dance is a brighter flash of blue against the sky. A kingfisher hovers to aim his dagger beak before diving, swift as an arrow, to pick a stickleback from beneath the water, then away to where his new-found mate sits cheeping, awaiting her wedding breakfast. The newly joined pair, their tryst sealed with a stickleback, speed across the meadow to the streamside and the hole in the sandbank which will be home for the glossy white clutch of eggs the hen will lay at the top of a 2 ft tunnel.

In the violet patch in the copse above the stream there is movement as pinholes appear in the heart-shaped leaves, tiny holes made by the horny mandibles of the freshly hatched silver-washed fritillary cater-pillars; they have spent their winter hidden in the bark of a nearby oak waiting for the warm air and the beckoning sun to call them out.

April is the month when countless millions of insects are hatching, and not only insects; tiny mites, spiderlike creatures of this primitive family, struggle for survival in a micro-world of hunter and hunted. The red–spider mite, so feared by fruit and vegetable growers, hatches from its red eggs laid in the bark of a twisted fruit free and scurries along the woody highway looking for newly opening leaves from

White admiral larva

Thrush feeding young

which it will suck the sap, the tree's life stream. Other mites will prey upon it, in turn, struggling to keep the balance.

Apple trees are also the home of the codling moth larvae, which hatch from overwintered eggs at this time of year and make their way to the tips of the apple shoots where the blossom buds are slowly unfurling. When the blossom has been visited by the bees and the tiny apple is set, the codling eats its way into the developing fruit to spend the spring and early summer gorging on an ever-increasing food supply until it is large enough to undergo the metamorphosis which will end in its emergence as a perfect moth.

Many apples are ruined by the attentions of this creature, which leaves a characteristic hole in the skin of the apple as it leaves to pupate. But it is not only harmful insects that emerge just now. Butterfly eggs are hatching, and the pupae of the tiny small blue and argus butterflies are almost ready to burst from their hiding-places among the grass stems where they have resisted the ravages of winter.

Buttercups spring from dormant roots and spread over the springing turf, eager to set seed before they are overshadowed by tall grasses. The meadow is coming alive and not even the late frosts will stop the new growth.

In the hedgerows, the birds that will depend on the insects, wait and warm their eggs while the food supply grows in the sun. The long-tailed tits no longer forage the hawthorn for food in family parties; they are paired now, and seek out the choicest lichen and spiders' webs to weave a ball of delicate strength, lined with horsehair or wool from the fieldside wire, in which to lay their tiny fragile eggs.

The bustle of activity is as though all the creatures were getting ready for a party – the Survival of the Species Ball, where all must be turned out in their finest attire or they will not be invited to participate in the game next year. Attend they must, for each plant and animal, each insect and spider, is as a brick to a building, each one dependent on another for its survival. Predator and prey depend on the links in the chain remaining unbroken. There is a balance in nature which, left to itself, works quite well even though the scales do not always hang level. Where there is excess production there will follow an increase in consumers until the equilibrium is restored.

The ultimate arbitrators in this game of survival are microscopic; the various diseases of plants and animals step in to restore the balance when all other methods fail. At the end of April the pans of the scales are still being balanced as the pace of life accelerates up the hill of the year.

8

MAY

If October is the crown prince of the year, then May surely must be the queen. If April is the month of pregnancy, May is the month of birth. All around is evidence of new life and promise; reality after expectancy, satisfaction after desire. The countryside is buzzing, and up and down the land the blossom is upon the branches, new buds are breaking from the protection of their cases and the leaves on the hawthorn mist the remaining hedgerows with green.

In the woods the floor is swept clear for the entrance of the ballet of the bluebells, a sheer delight and a tree-to-tree carpet of colour, providing a harvest of nectar for the bees as well as a feast for the human eye. The misty blue avenues between the columns of a beech wood conjure up visions of a cathedral, and in the imagination of the onlooker it needs only the sound of an organ playing Bach's Toccata and Fugue to complete the effect. Such is the magic of bluebells.

On the hillsides above the Medway estuary in Kent, the appearance of the bluebell is heralded by a less orchestral sound: the raucous cries of herons in their tree nests in the Nature Conservancy reserve at High Halstow rent the air. Here you can climb up frail ladders to treetop hides and commune with the reptilian-looking young born in this ancient heronry as they scream with hunger at their returning parents.

For centuries the heron has played its part in the life of England. In the past it was a quarry for the royal falconers, for whom it was deemed the highest prize and the greatest test of their falcon's skill, but in modern times it lives a shadowed life of contrasts. On the one hand it is protected on nature reserves and on the other it is persecuted as a foe of the fish farmer and river owner.

Heron

Although herons have some protection under the law, this is of minimal value and affords them no immunity on private land, where tales of herons spearing and damaging fish are produced as an excuse for destroying them. It has taken the heron millions of years to evolve as a master-fisherman and it is unreasonable for us to expect it to ignore such easily obtainable food. Killing the heron for doing what comes naturally is as morally indefensible as putting up a bird table and then shooting the blue tits when they come to the nut baskets. Herons have no moral judgement, they are not aware of 'ownership'; they are only aware of their need for food.

With the blossom comes the particular butterfly which typifies the countryside in May, the orange tip. A bustling flash of colour which has struggled from its thorn-shaped pupal case and now patrols a regular beat along the foaming beds of cow-parsley flowers, seeking the sombre female whose white wings lack the brilliant orange wingtips. The females do not fly over the lane margins sparring with other insects, but sip nectar awaiting their mates.

Where local authorities have reduced the cutting of roadside verges as an economy measure, many species of butterflies have increased, and the orange tip seems to have benefited more than most. All over southern England it can be seen on the wing, adding colour to the country scene. One of the food plants of this charming insect is 'jack by the hedge' or 'garlic mustard', so called because the leaves smell strongly of garlic when crushed in the hand. After the female has been fertilised by the male she lays her single eggs on the underside of the flower buds and on hatching, the larva's first meal is its own eggshell; then it begins to feed on the flower buds. The tiny green caterpillars are unsociable little beasts and will attack and eat their brothers and sisters until only one insect is left on the plant; but fortunately more uncut verges means more garlic-mustard plants, and in consequence a greater chance for the single caterpillars to reach maturity.

Most of our native butterflies are specific in their choice of food plant, and one of the other early spring insects, a much rarer one, is the Duke of Burgundy fritillary whose caterpillars must feed on the leaves of the cowslip. Unfortunately increased cultivation of fields right up

Female orange tip on cuckoo flower

Garlic mustard and wild forget-me-not

to the woodside has meant that both insect and cowslip have become scarcer in recent years.

Cowslips and primroses are closely related, members of the primula family, and will sometimes hybridise, the offspring of the union being intermediate in character. However, the primrose varies in colour on its own account, seeming to vary with the amount of sunshine falling upon it and the mildness of the climate. In Britain, the full-blown flowers on sunny banks are usually the colour of clotted cream, and in the West Country in May huge clumps of primroses on the hillsides give the impression that a clumsy dairymaid has passed that way. In the very south and in the Channel Islands grows a pink variety, and even further south on the continent, primroses can be a deep shade of red, like some of our garden varieties.

Many of our native plants can be found either in or near the woods and hedges, and in May in the hedge bottoms and on banksides wood anemones begin to appear. These delicate whitish flowers are much associated with fairies and when seen swaying in the gentle breeze along a sunken lane it is not hard to imagine fairy dancers.

The month of May is characterised by a wealth of wild flowers and the flowering of many native trees, and one of the most spectacular of these is the horse chestnut. It is decked with a mass of new green leaves and pink or white spire-shaped blossoms which flower on the tips of the branches, and later yield the conkers still loved by small boys.

Lamb's tails

Quite a few trees flower almost without our noticing. The alder with its catkins is not as showy as the horse-chestnut blossom, nor is the ash, whose brown flowers must set to become the mass of winged seeds we see later in the year. Tree flowers are often a quiet brown or green, although even with the natives there are exceptions: the field maple gilds its branches with a gloss of golden flowers inviting insects to come for a free meal.

In parks and town gardens local authorities and private individuals have planted exotic species of the cherry and apple family. These plants are purely ornamental, few of them having any commercial value as timber. However they are of suitable size for town sites and their branches, covered in snowy-white or candy-pink blossom almost to unreality, enliven otherwise dull surroundings in some of our towns. Because they are not native to these islands, few insects depend on their foliage for food, although the communal catterpillars of the lackey moth will colonise the flowering cherry and indeed they find the tree so much to their liking they strip the leaves from it. Not only the lackey moth appreciates it, for in the depths of each flower hides a tiny drop of nectar and it is on this nectar that the early bee depends.

The honey bees are beginning to work now, with the industry attributed to bees. In the hive the queen lays her eggs to swell the ranks of the sterile workers and make the most of the flower harvest. The bumble bees too are crashing around from flower to flower, garnering nectar, particularly from the secret bugle flower whose complicated petals will only open to reveal their treasure to the insect who knows their combination. Nature, incredibly, has evolved creatures and plants to take exclusive advantage of one another for their mutual benefit, and amongst the Maytime flowers lurk the masters of camouflage matching their form and colouration to plants and flowers, disguising themselves so effectively that visiting insects are not aware of their presence until the lurking flower springs out on its eight legs revealing itself to be a spider.

Moorhen chicks in nest

Spiders, those unlovely hunters, have evolved from primitive ancestors going back at least 400 million years. It is conjectured that the success of the spider clan forced other insects into the air in the first place, and fortunately for them no known spider has developed the ability to fly. Young spiders, though, do take to the air; indeed they were the first exponents of hang-gliding. On a day when the breeze is gentle the spiderlets climb to the top of a grass stem and spin their own hang glider from a silken thread. Then they float off into the wide world to establish their own territory, a tough assignment for them because for every square foot of land in the country there are, reputedly, about ten spiders of various species; it is one of nature's miracles that any young spiders ever reach maturity.

However, there is no waste in the natural world. Every creature and plant has its use in the cycle of life and death.

Most birds take advantage of the superabundance of insects to provide their growing young with protein, but there is one notable exception – the pirate of the bird world, who sits on a fence post and cuckoos to the world and his future mate, while she in turn watches the reed warblers weaving their intricate nests among the phragmites reed stems.

Cuckoo

The cuckoo is one of the characters of the bird world. Even its food requirements are unique. Of all the tasty morsels which nature makes available in the burgeoning countryside during May, the cuckoo chooses only the hairy caterpillars of moths, the very creatures which other birds and animals ignore because the caterpillars' hair irritates their throat lining. These caterpillars have a restricted season of growth so the cuckoo must match its migration to the availability of its special food supply.

Above the phragmites stems the air is a-twitter with returning swallows and house martins who have also timed their arrival to coincide with the explosion of free-flying insects. Of all the avian travellers the swallow is the most welcome. The arrival of the first cuckoo may merit a letter to *The Times*, but the appearance of the first swallow heralds the summer. It returns each year with unerring accuracy to the very place, sometimes even the very barn, in which it was reared. With these fast fliers comes the ultimate master of flight, a predator of the swallow, the sickle-winged hobby, returning to its nesting sites in the heathlands of Dorset and Hampshire and the downland of the Chilterns.

Hobbys need quiet and seclusion to nest and rear their young. They are creatures who find it hard to come to terms with increasing urbanisation. Also they are at the top of a food chain and have suffered badly from the effect of persistent insecticides, not only in this country but also on the long migration routes to and from Africa. The developing countries still use persistent pesticides such as DDT for the control of disease-carrying insects, and swallows accumulate enough of these poisons in their bodies to affect the nesting success of the hobby when it returns to us.

The population of hobbys in England is probably no more than 100 pairs and these are restricted to the southern counties, for they need heath and downland for successful breeding. They are matchless fliers, freest of a race of free creatures. Of all the falcons the hobby reigns supreme in flight. In the days when falconry was popular, the hobby was the ladies' falcon and it was flown against larks and swallows; it can even fly down a swift. The male hobby, as with all falcons, is known as the tiercel. Only the female is called a falcon. In the spring evenings they perform a riveting courting display: the male flies past the female at full pelt, dropping food – often a small bird – which she promptly catches. As well as small birds hobbys catch insects, which they eat on the wing, holding the insect in the fist of the foot. For sheer spectacle there is nothing to beat the dashing flight of these birds.

Since the war the treatment of land used to grow grass for hay has changed. The old hay meadows are now almost only a memory and grazing land for dairy cattle these days bears a different flora, both in numbers and species. Many of the plants in a traditional meadow did not have a direct food value, but they played an important part in preserving the balance of nutrients; some of these now have to be added in the form of artificial plant food.

The most popular grass grown as a fodder crop is a variety of common rye grass. It is believed to be the earliest type cultivated and sown as a crop and there are records of its use in the fifteenth century. It is a luxuriant plant, and a field of rye grass sways and ripples in a breeze like a gentle sea. It has now mainly superseded the old mixed species grown, which consisted of brome grasses and several varieties of meadow grasses each one specially adapted to the soil type they inhabited. Treatment with artificial fertilisers did not benefit them and the more vigorous-growing plants smothered and overtook the highly adapted species.

Common field grasshopper

Stitchwort

Above all it is the loss of plant species specific to pasture land which has changed the face of the English meadow. Only in the counties of Dorset and Hampshire and in parts of Devon is there any quantity of old grazing pasture remaining. In Dorset especially, the unpolled cows munch their way knee-deep in Maytime flowers. Traditional meadowland here has not seen the ploughshare for centuries; indeed in the Bridport area the fields on the steep coombes show evidence of pre-Enclosure Acts strip agriculture, and stepped strips, remains of the lynchets made by medieval peasants, rise like terraces on the hillsides. These terraces support a plentitude of wild plants, again many of which our forefathers harvested for medicinal purposes.

The orchid family are all highly specialised in soil and climatic requirements, and it takes years for orchid plants to reach maturity and flower. Because they are so attractive to look at they were frequently dug up for planting in domestic gardens before the Protection of Wild Creatures and Wild Plants Act. They will grow in gardens, but because of their specialisation they do not thrive and will eventually die, often because the gardener has fed them with artificial plant food, which they cannot tolerate. In the main they are plants of impoverished soils and too much nitrogen kills them.

The earliest orchid to appear is the twayblade, an unspectacular plant with green flowers on a long green stem. The name twayblade means two-leafed and the flowering stem rises from two pancake-shaped leaves, the flower cluster carrying a host of green flowers each with two strap-like petals below the lip. The other orchid of the spring is the early purple, a delicate lilac-coloured flower rising on a long stalk from a pair of strap-shaped fleshy leaves, black-blotched on their dark green surface. These leaf spots can cause confusion with the common spotted orchid, which mainly blooms in early June, although some do appear in certain localities in late May. Both of these orchids are natives of alkaline soils and will not tolerate an acid environment.

Along the edge of the meadow, young rabbits bumble their blunt noses into the fresh green pasture, blissfully unaware of danger which lurks behind every bush and in the cloudless blue, where watchful buzzards circle the thermals looking down from their lofty vantage point with eyes ten times keener than man's. The buzzard chicks are now reaching the stage where they will stand on the edge of their bulky nest-platform of twigs, trying out their stubby wings. They are still flecked with the down which protects them whilst their coat of strong brown feathers is growing. Their appetite has kept pace with their development; when they were helpless chicks the female plucked them scraps of meat from animal carcasses she brought back to the nest, feeding them delicately with her sharp hooked beak. Now they are strong enough to help themselves and they fight, mew and bicker over the delicacies brought in by their parents.

Although the buzzard is one of the largest of our birds of prey, it is not as efficient a killing-machine as its mighty relative the golden eagle, which can stoop like a feathered thunderbolt, skimming the surface of the glens, to take a full-grown hare at the run. The buzzard is far better adapted to eat carrion and smaller creatures. When myxomatosis struck the rabbit population the buzzards had a field day, but only whilst the disease was rife. During the spring following the peak epidemic, broods of buzzards all over the country failed to reach maturity due to lack of food. With its weak feet the buzzard is not well adapted to gripping and killing, and without baby rabbits for prey it drastically declined in numbers, vanishing from traditional haunts. Rabbits have developed some immunity to myxomatosis by now, and

Buzzard

as their numbers have began to recover, the buzzard too has again begun to spread from the West Country and the North into areas as close to London as Oxfordshire.

Also in Oxfordshire a few pairs of nightingales can be heard singing in the coppiced hazel. These birds are denizens of dense woodland and their decline is almost directly attributable to the ending of the practice of coppicing. This practice created habitat for a host of creatures requiring dense cover rather than deep mature forest. Medium-sized trees, usually oak or hazel, were felled in such a way that the root was not killed, enabling the stump to send up a spray of strong new shoots. In the past these were harvested for tanning bark, for charcoal for ironworks, for poles for hurdles and farm implements. Hazel was used for various farm items and was the ideal material for hurdles and sheep fences. It is easy to weave when wet and immensely strong and resilient when dry, and therefore was long used to make strong baskets for farm produce.

Coppicing first came about because of the demands of the charcoal burner in the sixteenth century, when the destruction of trees to feed the demands of rapidly growing industries and population led to a timber famine. At this time, too, more woodland was being enclosed for hunting and parkland, so the charcoal burners and tanners, without efficient means of transport had to start farming trees instead of depleting the natural stock. The method probably happened accidentally, when inefficiently felled trees and saplings were seen to grow a forest of side shoots at great speed. Undamaged root systems, initially developed to feed and support a whole tree, when left with only small branches to nourish, will send them up very quickly, in ten years or so, a felled tree could again produce a harvestable crop of small timber, a discovery that must have been a life-saver to the woodmen of those days. Over the centuries the rotation of felling and coppicing was brought to a fine art, which is especially evident in the oak woodland on the edge of Dartmoor. The moor itself has been largely denuded of its once dense forest, but in woods like the National Trust's at Hembury, near the monastery of Buckfast, there is recent evidence of this practice, and the oak woodland there supports a healthy shrub flora and fauna.

The decline in the use of charcoal as a fuel, and the development of synthetic substitutes for oak-bark tanning for leather, has almost ended the usefulness of coppicing, so the shoots thrown up by the stumps have gone on to reach the dimensions of small trees, changing the habitat from dense underbrush to open woodland. Another creature that liked the coppice woodland has also declined – the gentle dormouse.

In the south-eastern quarter of Britain is a different type of woodland with different species: trees whose wood was of little value for charcoal and whose bark did not yield the quantities of tannin necessary for the leather industry. The beech, for instance, is a structural timber, useful for building furniture only when it is mature. The beeches of our forefathers' time were probably not as mighty as the grey columns now gracing our countryside, rooted in the chalk. Transport and motive power were not easily available to deal with a tree weighing many tons and measuring 60 ft or so to the crown, so trees would have been harvested when they were half the size of those we now know. Evidence of a timber famine in the mid-seventeenth century can be found by checking the age of these trees. Many of the oaks and beeches on the Chiltern hills are about 200 years old and must have been planted to replace timber cut down at that time.

There is, however, some relic woodland remaining, which gives an echo of the environment surrounding our ancestors. It covers only small areas and is usually to be found in terrain where, until this century, access and removal of timber was difficult. Much of the ancient forest, too, is composed of small and stunted trees – the forest's salvation, as they were uneconomic to fell, though many were coppiced. There have been occasions when it has been suggested that an ancient oak wood should be felled in order to plant conifers, and in the Powerstock forest in Dorset a start was actually made. Fortunately a band of conservationists were able to stop the felling and part of the original forest still stands – a reminder of what can happen if vigilance is not maintained.

The British Isles, of course, were covered in forest until relatively recently. Many mainland birds and mammals are woodland species, and birds like the robin which we have come to regard as garden-species, are not so in Europe. There they are confined to dense woodland, sharing the shyness and retiring disposition of their cousin the nightingale. While our extrovert garden robin perches on the spade waiting for worms, in Europe the robins are skulking birds of the bramble thickets. The blackbird, too, has the anatomy of a typical woodland bird, strong rounded wings and a long tail to enable it to manoeuvre in a restricted environment. Only in this country is it evident in such large numbers around the towns, thanks largely to the efforts of the human population who feed them in the winter and whose gardens provide nesting sites.

The fact that numbers of British birds and animals are basically forest creatures becomes more obvious at this time of year, and the value of hedgerows as substitute breeding habitat for them is brought home. Hedgerows are a fairly recent innovation, the majority having been planted for a mere 400 years or so, although some date back to Saxon times. Owing to the dense forest cover over much of the land up to the Middle Ages there was little need for hedges in most areas.

The patchwork of fields imposed by the Enclosure Acts produced thousands of miles of hedges which displaced forest creatures were able to colonise, but with the hedges now disappearing at the rate of 2,000 miles per year the habitat for many familiar birds and animals is being removed. They find it too big a jump for them to adapt from hedgerow to open farmland; it would require a change in both body shape and basic habits.

Man, who has brought about this shift in the natural order of things, has no such problems of adaptation to a changed environment. There is a commonly held belief that prehistoric man inhabited a world which was hostile, cold, grey and uncomfortable, and that the modern world is a far better place in which to live. In certain respects, especially when we consider modern medicine, this is true, but the environment which our primitive ancestors inhabited was like the

Garden of Eden compared with the countryside today. Their world was often a riot of colour, a place teeming with all the necessities of their simple lives. Deer and wild ox grazed in the clearings and a million wild flowers greeted their gaze when they rubbed the sleep from their eyes on spring mornings.

The water was always sweet and uncontaminated by anything other than the minerals which leached from the rocks naturally. The air was full of the buzz of insects and the song of birds. There was no shortage of food, even in winter, as there were few men around. Ancient man was at least at one with his environment, part of the natural scheme of things, a fact illuminated by the cave paintings found in Spain and France. He had the time to admire and copy the beauties of nature. And he could produce artefacts which ultimately made him both master and slave of his environment. For instance it takes hours of painstaking effort to produce a stone knife, but the energy used is supplied from within the craftsman and is soon replaced by food, a readily renewable source. A metal knife, on the other hand, is no more efficient at cutting than a stone one – it simply has a longer working life; but its production requires the consumption of a hundred times more energy and non-renewable natural commodities.

We tend to look down on the shambling figure of our dim and distant past, but environmentally he was our superior.

As May dances on, the pace of the natural world reaches a crescendo. In the quiet of the wood the fresh green fronds of the bracken curl up from the warm earth in between a mist of delicate woodmelick grasses. A fallow doe has just given birth to a spotted fawn, whose dappled coat matches to perfection the pattern of May sunlight trickling through the bright newspun green of the tree canopy over head. The young fawn will stay where its mother puts it, for the dapple camouflage is only of value while it lies still. If it were to stumble around the undergrowth it would broadcast its presence to all and sundry by sight, scent and smell, a deadly combination of sensory stimuli. The real predator of deer no longer stalks the woods on soft pads: the last wolf was killed in Sutherland a long time ago. But the deer have not forgotten this extinct foe.

The fox too preys on fawns, but the period during which the young deer are at risk is very short indeed. Usually only a minute number of living young deer or lambs fall prey to reynard. Far more often the fox scavenges those that are dead and still-born. Observations of foxes in fields where there are sheep, even sheep with lambs, show that ewes do not regard the fox as a threat to them or their young. There are exceptions to every rule and no doubt the fox takes a lamb occasionally but this is not a regular occurrence. Likewise with young deer.

The most dangerous period in a fawn's life comes some weeks later, when it is more mobile and running with its mother. Then it becomes prey to a far more dangerous menace, the motor car. Cars probably kill more young deer than anything else, and it is a problem which is hard to overcome; fallow deer, especially, jump great heights and can clear fences and hedges with ease, giving the unsuspecting motorist no time to take avoiding action. Yet in one way too many of those motorists are at fault: having hit a deer they do not check to see whether the animal is dead or injured. Is this through fear of prosecution, or merely fear of the animal itself? Such cases result in a great deal of unnecessary suffering to animals.

Cowslip

In recent years there appears to have been a slight shift in the weather pattern of northern Europe which has resulted in spring arriving several weeks later than we had thought to be the average. The plants of the roadside and woodland margins open later and continue to flower for a longer period. The primrose and cowslip exhibit this tendency and both of them are much reduced in their distribution. One likely cause is that they are quite often dug up by the roots for replanting in town gardens, but another factor, which is now being considered, is the climate's influence on certain plants which are at the northern limit of their distribution in these islands. Quite a small

149

shift in the weather pattern would have a marked effect on them.

Some of the insects in the British Isles, too, are at the northern edge of their range; although the habitat is similar to that on the continent, the island climate, with usually wet mild winters, does not suit them. Both the long-tailed and the short-tailed blue butterflies come into this category. They are common in Europe right up to the Channel coast, but are only rare vagrants in this country. Although the short-tailed blue has bred here it will not overwinter, and it is unlikely that it will ever become a breeding species in any numbers.

At the other end of the scale is the Camberwell beauty, a member of the same family as our peacock and red admiral. This insect is a native of Scandinavia and not uncommonly visits this country in timber imports from Sweden and Norway. Its dark wings with daffodil-yellow borders make it a most beautiful creature. Its food plant, willow, abounds here, but the larvae have been found only on a few occasions and unfortunately the damp British winters are not to its liking. Its distribution is world-wide and in the USA it is known as the mourning cloak, because of the deep brownish-purple wing colouring.

Now is the time to make provision for butterflies in the garden. It is a great temptation to tidy every last corner and remove any plant remotely resembling a weed, but it is worth while leaving a small patch where nettles can grow as these are the food plant of a wide variety of our more attractive breeding butterflies, such as the small tortoiseshell and peacock. The planting of sedum and michaelmas daisies and the 'butterfly bush', buddleia, will ensure that later in the year the garden will be full of butterfly-attracting flowers. Not only will these plants be visited by day; the nightshift of the insect world will be on the wing too, for multitudes of moths abound in every garden. Compared with the profusion of species of these velvety creatures, the numbers of day-flying members of the Lepidoptera family are surprisingly small. Moths have made a niche for themselves in the hours of darkness, and the study of moths by the general public has therefore been limited. Yet they are among the most fascinating of insects, with a lifestyle specially adapted to a low-light environment and life histories which make even the most interesting butterfly seem almost dull by comparison.

Moths live in a world of smells of infinite delicacy and their compound eyes pick up ultra-violet light like a radar scanner, enabling them to home in on plants whose flowers reflect colours in this spectrum which we cannot see. Sadly they have a poor public image, simply because the larvae of one or two species choose to eat spun cloth and feathers – so the whole family come under suspicion! Without the wide-ranging family of moths, the bird life of this country would be far less varied, because moth caterpillars provide 80 per cent of the food for young song birds.

For sheer beauty there are few creatures who can hold a candle to a moth and the well-known attraction of these insects to a candle flame is yet another example of their magnificent adaptation to a lightless life. It is conjectured that moths navigate by the light of the moon and the light-wave lengths of a candle flame give the impression of a substitute moon, around which the insect tries to navigate, often disastrously.

Hawkmoth

As the month of May closes, the apple trees in the gardens and orchards are clothed with pink and white as the blossom reaches maturity, and the bees, now in full spate, dash and hum from flower to flower exchanging pollen from one tree to the next, fertilising the autumn's fruit.

In the Chiltern woods the canopy is misted with white as if the trees were celebrating a wedding, as the wild cherry decks its french-polished branches with blossom. Most of these trees are set by birds, that is to say that the fruit stones were deposited in bird droppings and there took root. This is a tree particularly of the chalk downland, especially Hertfordshire and Bedfordshire, and some of them grow to great size and form a large proportion of the stand. Wild cherry timber is beautiful and very strong with all the colours of a muted rainbow in its striped grain, ranging from green to pink and through all the intermediate shades to rich red. It is a difficult wood to work for it will twist and crack if sawn; yet treated as the craftsmen of old treated timber, it can be perfection for the furniture maker. The old method was to split or 'riven' the cherry log across its diameter with wedges, so that the worker would be left with triangles of wood from which all the twisting stress had been removed.

Like all native timber it needs seasoning for long periods to allow it to dry and become stable enough for working, and in order to avoid splitting the finished piece the wood is worked at an angle. In this way the full beauty of the straight bands of colour are shown to the best effect.

In common with most of the finest home-grown woods, cherry is prone to attack from wood-boring beetles, and a large proportion of old farmhouse furniture has succumbed to the depredations of this pest. Despite this, quite a number of fine chairs and settles made of cherrywood remain. Cherry was and still is one of the favourite timbers of the wood carver, because of the tight, straight grain, but of all wood available for carving, lime is the nearest to perfection in an English forest. Although relatively uncommon, the lime is much sought-after for carving even though the treatment necessary before working is long and arduous. It takes several years for the felled timber to reach a state of stability and hard dryness suitable for carving.

The famous carver Grinling Gibbons used lime wood for many of his most complex pieces, and it rewards the skilled artist with fine lines and sharp edges as no other material can. Screens and furniture in some of our most beautiful churches and cathedrals are executed in lime and oak, two woods complementary in texture and colour. Lime is not as resistant as oak to the ravages of woodworm and rot, but it is a durable material if it is kept dry and painted.

The humble woodworm, now on the wing as an adult beetle, has done much to shape the design of English country furniture, and a great number of the pieces which have come down to us from past centuries have features specially designed to resist its ravages. Old pieces were treated with red lead on the underside to poison the larvae before they could do their worst, and the fine joinery and heavy

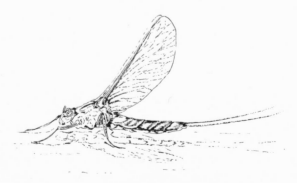

Mayfly

152

Swift

waxing of old furniture owes much to the attempts of the joiner to fill all the crevices where the beetle might lay its eggs.

Happily, there are other, more romantic, insects which fill the air of May. At the riverside the observer can see the first showing of the mayflies, gauzy creatures which flutter weakly at the water's edge drying their wings before taking off on their nuptial flight. The mass of mayflies on the water can make the normally wary trout lose their caution and even the deep-bodied mature trout, kings of the pools and streams, act like fry at mayfly time, dashing from fly to fly gulping their succulent bodies in a frenzy of feeding.

This is the time of year when even the biggest of trout can be taken with ease on any artificial dressing vaguely resembling a mayfly, but the hatch is not long in the air and soon, as the heat of June appears on the horizon of the morning sky, the mayfly is gone. Only a few spent creatures float in the quiet eddies and the surviving leviathans of the river again don their mantle of caution and sink beneath the edge of the waving ranunculus forest which springs from the bright gravel of the river bed.

The summer migrants have nearly all arrived now, and most of them have set up territories and are sitting on the first of their eggs. The last to arrive is one of the first to leave. This is the swift, the bird which spends its life on the wing, even sleeping as it flies. Swifts migrate in vast flocks, arriving on the Channel coasts like swarms of dancing gnats high up in the blue skies. Migration for them is not the epic journey undertaken by other migrants, for these birds are always in the air and move northwards with little effort, harvesting the growing insect population ahead of them.

They are very sensitive to changing atmospheric pressure and can sense an area of high pressure, or a front, miles away. The upwelling of air as the front approaches draws up insects into the atmosphere to the swift's advantage, and it times its arrival in this country to coincide with the mass hatchings of flying insects of the early summer. Without them the young swifts would not survive when they are hatched in the dark of church steeple or barn. The adult swift cannot take off from flat ground. Its long highly swept wings are designed for high-speed flight and have insufficient lift to raise the bird from the ground; its feet, which are tiny and far back on its body, cannot propel it forward with enough speed for take off. So the swift must nest in high places, where it can launch itself into the air, a medium in which it has total mastery.

9

JUNE

'Flaming' is the epithet generally ascribed to June and almost always June provides us with at least one miniature heatwave with temperatures well up into the 70s Fahrenheit.

June is also characterised by a great blooming of native wild plants. Now is the time when hedgerows and field margins, meadows and downs are ablaze with masses of flowers. The fields glow like yellow fire as the rape blooms, and in the woodland rides the blackberry flowers shine like stars against the deep glossy green of the leaves. On warm days, the summer air hums with a leisurely activity. Hoverflies hang stationary in the heat-shimmering air, along the hedges dog roses and eglantine deck the hawthorns with garlands and the convolvulus twists its embrace over the blackthorn and raises its white trumpets to the sky, where the swifts skirl and scream as they hurtle in pursuit of an aerial banquet of insects.

At the waterside swallows hawk, their long migration forgotten in the frantic search for food for their young who crouch, mouths agape, in the dry mud cups of their nests in old barns, whose beams have witnessed the upbringing of several hundred generations of swallows. In the corner of the barn where grey cobwebs hang like

Wild rose

dirty cardigans, downy grey barn-owl chicks peer at the comings and goings of the parent swallows, through the open doorway above the dry dusty straw where field mice scurry.

The cows, who once occupied these barns, now file into modern milking parlours where droning machinery has replaced the more leisurely hand milking which used to punctuate farm days. Hand milking is a delicate skill. Cattle will not take kindly to rough handling when their udders are full, and may refuse to let down their milk for the inexperienced or kick or press against a heavy-handed dairy man or maid. But there is something restful about hand milking, hard and tiring work though it is: the cattle exude a warm rich smell when they stand content in their stalls waiting for the hands of the milker to draw the foaming liquid from their udders, and the steady sound of munching as they eat from the manger adds to the peaceful effect.

One of my earliest memories is of walking, stick in hand, beside the publican of the Clovelly Inn, shouting at the sleek red Devon cows as they were brought up from the lower fields and along the lane which generations of men and cattle had indented. I used to think it was my high-pitched call of 'ai, ai, ai,' which brought the shambling red beasts up the steep lane, but the fact is that these gentle animals would perform the same journey without human help. If, as sometimes happened, their field gate was insecurely fastened, they would tramp up the hill unbidden to stand lowing outside the crumbling shippon waiting for the ministrations of the publican. Following the cows to milking was a most enjoyable pastime; the smell and mesmerising movement of their rumps, reminiscent of a sailor's swaying gait, imparted a sense of timelessness.

I was initiated into the gentle art of hand milking at such an early age I cannot remember not being able to do it; being small, if I sat on the three-legged stool my head only came level with the underside of the cow's belly, my eyes in line with the top of its udders. When my arms grew tired Sonny, the publican-cowman, would take over, continuing the pulsing swish of the milk into the shining bucket. Then I would sit in the straw with the farm cats waiting for a jet of sweet warm milk which Sonny would direct at our open mouths. The cats were more adroit at catching the milk, and also had the distinct advantage of being able to collect the spray on their coats and harvest it later when they washed their stiffened fur. I would often return home with my face fixed in a milk-stiffened mask and my blond hair waved in milky peaks. The shippon had witnessed such events for over 600 years;

Clovelly Inn

twice daily the cycle of milking had been taking place within the thick lime-washed cob walls.

The cycle of meadow plants into milk, milk into cream and cheese and butter, was still carried on as a matter of course in country districts right up to the 1940s. In Bratton, when the full milk pails were poured into a churn, through a filter which removed any floating dust and chaff, the milk was taken to cool in a large stone-flagged room at the back of the pub, a room that had seen the reception of milk for hundreds of years and had been especially designed for storing dairy products. Built partly below ground level it maintained its coolness even in the hottest weather.

Clotted cream, for which Devon is justly famous, was made here. Large enamel pans filled with fresh milk were set to stand undisturbed for at least twenty-four hours so that the butterfat would rise to the surface. Then, very carefully, these pans were taken into the huge kitchen, with its stone floor and long refectory table, for the milk to be scalded. It was never allowed to boil, just simmered for several hours until a thick crust of golden-yellow formed on the surface. The pans were then taken back to the dairy to cool.

It was a ploy of mine to try to call at a time when the cream was being taken from the pans, scooped carefully into china bowls with a large flat metal ladle. This was the raw material for butter, but I could usually persuade the publican's wife to give me a spoonful before it all went into the churn. Some of the left-over buttermilk was used for porridge, and this porridge, topped with cream, was the best in the world. The remaining buttermilk then went to the pigs on a nearby farm who happily slurped and snorted their way through it.

The life of these free-ranging pigs was, until their journey to the slaughterhouse, an idyllic one. Allowed to roam the fallow fields, they grubbed in the red earth for roots or whatever tickles a pig's fancy. Of all the farm animals, pigs are the greatest characters. They have a decided personality with facial expressions which can change, reflecting their moods. The pigs of the West of England used to be mainly blacks or saddlebacks, or occasionally the rich red-furred Tamworths, whose piglets look like furry sausages. Tamworths have quite small litters compared with the more refined breeds like the immense large whites, whose larger litters often perish under the bulk of the sow when she inadvertently lies on them. But the more rangy Tamworths tend their litters with care.

Pigs foraging in woodland are re-enacting a scene familiar in the English countryside for thousands of years. As cultivators, pigs have few equals; they will root and turn over the roughest scrub between the trees, leaving a fine level of fertilised tilth carpeted with rich green grass. Much of the common woodland in the Middle Ages was treated to the grubbing of pigs and the resulting green sward made good grazing for the peasants' cattle.

The June sunshine acts as a magnet for insects. The rides and meadows vibrate with their comings and goings and dragonflies helicopter over the reeds in search of prey. Sleek spotted flycatchers flit from their watching posts to snap up passing gnats until their beaks are bristling with food for their young. The urgency of hunting in the food-rich air is compelled by the need to feed a new generation of creatures.

Skylark

Out on the hayfields the fluffy marbled chicks of that farmland wader the lapwing are running between the forest stems of grass, providing an easy meal for a hovering kestrel, whilst the parent bird performs desperate aerobatics, finally resorting to the stratagem of feigning a broken wing to lure the mouse falcon away from its young. Unaware of this drama a skylark ascends on fluttering wings, pouring out a liquid song until it is a mere speck in the sky above, and in the woods at the edge of the field wood-pigeons bill and coo to one another. The undergrowth is alive with tiny scurrying creatures.

Beetles are delving in the leaf litter and shrews grow fat on the beetles as the time of plenty is upon the countryside.

In the bramble thickets wrens flit to and fro, their nests hung like a child's lost ball in the depths of the prickly stalks. Sometimes the wren's nest bulges under the weight of an interloper for which it was never designed, a young cuckoo who squeaks forlornly from its cramped quarters while the frantic foster parents shuttle backwards and forwards with food. It is astonishing that the wrens do not recognise the interloper as not being one of their own kind, but the open beak of the baby cuckoo is a magnet and they must keep trying to satisfy the insatiable appetite.

The density of the burgeoning vegetation so cuts down the light on the woodland floor that the creatures of the night can come and go as they please even in day-time. Woodmice squeak and scurry in the artificial twilight, protected from the owl by night and the kestrel by day, but their numbers are kept in check by the demands of young weasels, who skitter and scamper at the mouth of their mouse-hole home. As for many young wild creatures, play is a necessary preliminary to the serious business of finding enough food to stay alive. The weasel family is a cohesive unit staying together for a considerable time after the young are weaned. It is not unusual to see family groups hunting a hedgerow together in late June and early July and even in the midst of these hunting expeditions the younger members of the group will break off to play. Though so fast in movement, they are very curious and can be called to within a few feet by imitating a mouse distress call, a noise which can be made by humans by sucking air through pursed lips. This curiosity has led many a weasel to finish up on a keeper's gibbet. Much as they are despised as slinking killers of game, they can be regarded as a friend to the farmer, for there are no more efficient ratters than weasels. Their presence under the floor of a barn will certainly rapidly clear out any rats far more effectively than a farm cat.

Many years ago I witnessed a tussle between these two masters of mousing where the cat was definitely worsted. A weasel had killed a particularly large rat and was attempting to take it to a spot beneath the barn where her young were closeted. It was one of those barns where the floor was supported by mushroom-shaped stone columns designed to foil the entry of rats. As the weasel returned with her prize she was observed by a cat, sunning itself on the edge of a projecting beam. The cat's eyes were drawn to the movement and she crouched as the heavily laden weasel drew nearer. Having no fear of the tiny

Weasel at mouse-hole

hunter, the cat sprang, but despite the speed and suddenness of the attack the weasel saw it coming and, temporarily dropping the rat, sprang to the defence of her meal. She met the cat coming down and fastened her teeth in its outstretched paw. With a scream of shock the cat shook its paw to rid itself of the weasel and tried to bite its adversary. The weasel let go, but only to bury her sharp teeth in the cat's cheek.

Like Rikki Tikki Tavvi the weasel hung on; the cat decided discretion was the better part of valour and tried to run off. But the weasel would not let go, releasing her hold only when the pair were halfway across the yard. She stood chittering in triumph at the fleeing moggie, then returned to the rat and dragged it under the barn to her waiting young.

The weasel's small size does not prevent it from tackling prey as large as a full-grown rabbit, but this is rare and at this time of year there is ample food available in the shape of unwary fledglings who, having left the nest, advertise their presence by calling to their parents.

Bats flit and squeak in the evening air, reaping the harvest of the night. High above the streams and lakes noctules hawk at high level, taking the large insects, whilst the smaller bats fill other niches, collecting insects from just above the water and around the woodland edge. Their echo-location system is so refined they can distinguish between a small stone and a beetle in flight, and although they can be fooled into approaching if you throw a stone into the air they will turn

Bugle

away before they reach it. If the same experiment is done with a beetle, the bat will home in and take it before it can fall to the ground. Obviously they have evolved a system which can detect the density of an object as well as its presence. The sheer complexity of the range of sounds that must be received to gain this information almost defies description.

Recent investigations, though, have shown that as well as producing perfumes called feramones, some moths can emit sounds which confuse even bats. These are high-pitched clicks and squeaks which jam the bat's detection system.

Most signals in nature are those of attraction rather than defence, and visual stimuli are very important, especially in the interplay

162

between flowers and the insects which pollinate them. Many flowers guide incoming pollinators, outlining the entry point to the nectaries, showing them where to land and which direction to take. Certain colours are more inviting to insects than others. Low-growing plants like the bugle are attractive to quite a few invertebrates although the flowers are small: their shade of bluish-purple seems to be irresistible for butterflies and bees alike. The fact that there are so few truly red flowers seems to indicate that most insects cannot distinguish this hue. It has been proved that they have eyes capable of detecting the ultra-violet frequencies of the spectrum, and the moth-attracting devices, used by entomologists for census purposes, incorporate a lamp which emits this wavelength of light. It is more than likely that some of the day-flying members of the insect world have the same ability, and hence the predominance of blue or purple in the flowers most attractive to them. Once drawn to the flower, whether by colour or scent, a plentiful supply of nectar will encourage exploration and pollination.

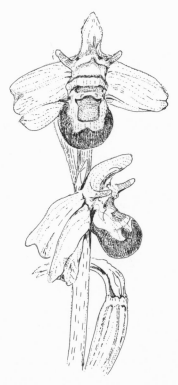

Bee orchid

163

Our native orchids are mainly reddish-purple or mauve in colour and are fertilised by insects seeking nectar, but some use mimicry to attract. The bee-orchid's flower is a marvellous imitation of the bumble bee *terrestris*, and consequently it is this species which visits the flower most often.

Some of the plants in the old-fashioned cottage garden, such as snapdragons and those plants with complex flowers, need to be visited by insects with a particular body shape and sufficient weight to open the lip of the flower, in order for pollination to be successful; and a long tongue is also needed to reach the hidden nectary. This type of plant is plentiful in the countryside and toadflax is one of them. It gives a bright splash of yellow to the banks and belongs to the family of legumes (peas). This vast army of plants includes flowers like lupins, and meadow and heath plants like the vetches, clover and the spiky gorse. All these plants have symbiotic bacteria in their root systems which fix free nitrogen in the soil, so making it available to other plants as food. In consequence of this remarkable property they are vital to the maintenance of fertility in the soil.

Large white on ox-eye daisy

Large blue on wild thyme

Because there is a superabundance of growing things at this time, there is also a superabundance of creatures; but not all those we have in our countryside are flourishing. Some have over-specialised and suffered for it. One such is the large blue, a butterfly with the most bizarre life history imaginable. This insect has always been confined to the southern half of the country and though now protected by law it is very rare, breeding in only a few sites. It is on the wing during the months of June and July, and lays its eggs on the flowers of wild thyme, growing on hillsides near the sea on the Devon and Cornish coasts. When they hatch, the tiny grubs make their first meal from their own eggshell, then begin to feed on thyme flowers. This idyllic existence continues until the caterpillar is half-grown, when wanderlust comes over it. It creeps down the plant stem and on to the ground to search for ants of a particular species. A type of red ant is attracted by a honey gland on the caterpillar, and duly picks it up and takes it to the colony. Here the caterpillar is milked of its honey, like a cow. However, the caterpillar repays its captor by eating the ant larvae in the nest before going cosily into hibernation for the winter. When it wakes up it resumes eating ant larvae, then hangs itself up and changes into a pupa, still in the ants' brood-chamber. Later it emerges as the perfect butterfly, to start the incredible cycle all over again.

Because the particular ants on which the large blue depends have become less numerous recently, and the butterfly itself is rare anyway, in the normal order of things the chances of the caterpillar finding the correct ant are pretty low. Sadly it is possible that this lovely and ususual creature may become extinct in the not too distant future. There is a Large Blue Preservation Society, and the Nature Conservancy Council have protected areas where the large blue can fly undisturbed by man, but it does not seem to be responding to this care and the numbers continue to decline. Such is the danger of over-specialisation.

In the ponds, specialisation is mainly confined to what is needed for living in water. Many of the creatures who spend their larval stage in water are beginning to make the transition to life in the open air. Tadpoles have now become froglets, still with their tails, but froglets just the same. They have legs and bodies like their parents and soon the tail will be re-absorbed and the young frog will take its place on the land – away from the predators of the under-water world, but in a new and equally hostile environment, among the grasses and tall stems of the great hairy willow herb which rises far above them.

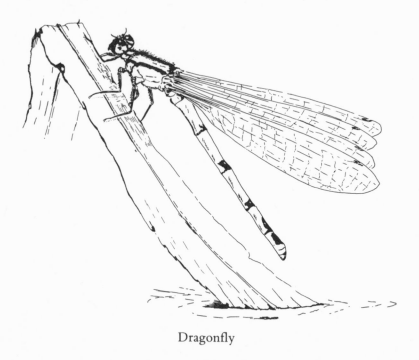

Dragonfly

The water is alive with plankton and algae and vibrates with the movements of a multitude of daphnia and cyclops. The dragonfly larvae are starting their journey up the reed stems to complete the transformation from unlovely bugs to iridescent aerial hunters. This creature has had hundreds of millions of years in which to perfect its shape and its skills, for dragonflies flew at the time the coal measures were laid down, and indeed their fossils have been found with the imprint of their gauzy wings still visible in rocks from coal mines. A very large number of pond inhabitants are just as they were aeons ago. Plankton, the rotifer and the amoeba are living prototypes of life as in early pre-history. A powerful magnifying glass will give an insight, but a microscope provides a window into another world.

A more advanced living fossil is also making its presence felt and heard both in garden and countryside. The hedgehogs are mating, filling the air with cries of love. The hedgehog woos by breathing heavily to his loved one and she melts under the spell of his breath. (Evolution has obviously removed from the scene any hedgehog with halitosis.) When mated the female hedgehog will bring her litter of

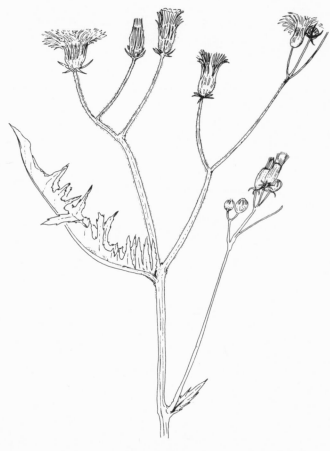

Hawksbeard

blind, soft-spined young into the world under a shed or a fallen tree, and she will tend and care for them lovingly even after their soft spines harden and life becomes prickly in the den. If a young one ventures out and loses its way its cries are heartrending and mother soon arrives to usher the straying urchin back to safety.

Hedgehogs have few enemies in the wild. Badgers are said to be able to open them with their strong claws, but fox cubs quickly learn to leave them well alone. Death in hibernation is the main control on their numbers, and the motor car has become a major predator, leaving the evidence of spiky corpses littering our roads. Despite the high mortality the hedgehog remains a success in the modern countryside.

All through the early spring and into June the grasses have been growing, converting minerals and nitrogen in the soil into sugar and sappy growth. As they come into flower, making the life of the hay-fever sufferers unbearable, plans are afoot to harvest them for hay. Of all the crops on the land, grass is the greatest single provider of nourishment for farm animals and wild creatures alike, both as hay for overwintering stock and as silage for cattle feed.

The process of haymaking still depends on good weather, as it has

Sickle and scythe

168

always done. Hay dried naturally in the open air is the sweetest and keeps better, and in the late spring farmers spend long hours looking skywards and listening to weather forecasts before embarking upon the hazardous job of haymaking. It is one of the greatest gambles in the farming calendar. A wet spell when the hay is cut can result in all the farmer's efforts producing a useless crop fit only for bedding. There is an art in assessing the crop too. Cut too soon, the resulting hay will be all water and fibre with low food value; cut too late, the hay will have too low a sugar content.

With modern highly mechanised methods, the drying crop is turned with a tractor-operated wheel hay turner, but a mere fifty years ago the whole process was extremely laborious, the grass being cut with a scythe and hook and the hay turned with forks. All the time this was taking place the farmer had to keep a weather eye open, praying for warm drying winds and sunshine.

The scythe, which was the main tool used for cutting hay, is superbly functional and effective for its task. The pattern has hardly changed over hundreds of years. In the hands of a novice it can appear a clumsy ill-designed combination of wood and metal – a device which would amputate the legs of the unwary. But in the hands of a practitioner it becomes a fluid living extension of the man. Sweeping forward and along with apparently little effort, the long sharp blade slides through the serried ranks of grass with a hiss, and the cut grass lies down with bowed head as if in deference to a superior. On first handling an ancient scythe it feels unwieldy and out of balance and with the strangely shaped stock the weighty steel blade seems predisposed to embed itself in the turf rather than flow over its surface; but once balanced the operation becomes logical, with the body of the operator as the pivot of the cutting machine.

The oldest scythes had blades with a ripple on the forward cutting edge which, when honed to sharpness, would slice through thistles and even reeds as though they were butter. After years of use the ripples on the blade became worn away by sharpening and the edge took on a razor-like keenness. Because farm scythes were so much used, the blades had to be replaced frequently and it is only on the few cottage-garden tools which have survived here and there that the ripple edge can sometimes still be seen.

Blades such as these were masterpieces of the blacksmith's art. The steel was forged and beaten in the way that swords and pikes were formed, hammered out from a billet of iron until the desired proportions were reached. The mere act of hammering the metal shaped its

Laid hedge in Somerset – a dying craft

structure into a springy, yet immensely strong, steel which, when tempered in a forge and sharpened on a wheel, reflected the skill of the craftsman. The ash shaft and handle doles were also bent and shaped by hand.

The tools which a man uses reflect his attitude to the job. The slim elegant curve of the hedger's sickle shows the care with which this craft was practised. The sheer cost of laying and maintaining hedges in the old labour-intensive way has brought its end on the bigger farms. It has been handed over to machines, which do not have either the precision necessary to trim a hedge properly or the adaptability and mechanical efficiency to lay one.

Laying a hedge is a craft which has been handed down from generation to generation, and apprentice hedgers would be taught how to cut the branches of shrubs and trees in such a way that they continue to grow thickly after being bent to form a stockproof barrier. The secret is to cut the growing branch so a proportion of the sap wood remains intact and attached to the main plant. In this way the branches can be woven into a living hurdle. The last ten years or so have seen the retirement of many of the older labourers on the land who possessed the skill, and because of the cost of replacement and training, contract workers are often now used for this work. But they are not specialised and do not have the proprietary pride of a permanent labour force.

In consequence laying hedges is mainly confined to the small farms that still maintain a pride, not only in the productivity of their land, but also in its appearance. Hedges are not only a utilitarian and visual amenity, they are the successors of the woodland that once covered these islands, vital for wildlife of all kinds. Insects, birds and mammals thrive in areas rich in hedgerows. The county of Dorset is a case in point: here there are more miles of rich hedgerows than almost anywhere else in the land.

Away from the countryside, all around the coastline, from the wild granite cliffs of Scotland to the jagged coast of north Cornwall and to the white chalks of the English Channel, rocky ledges croak with the sound of the seabirds re-enacting an age-old ritual. They have come in from their ocean beats to breed. On the islands off the Bristol Channel, for instance, strange birds fill the night air with wild unearthly screams. These are the Manx shearwaters, deep-ocean birds of the same family group as the albatross. As their name implies they skim or shear over the surface of the wild Atlantic on glider wings, riding the wind which strips the spume from the tops of the rollers. They pick up food from the water's surface, hardly ever coming to land except during the breeding season.

Manx shearwater

Because these birds live on the open ocean they have developed the ability to drink sea water and dispose of the salt so that their blood does not turn to brine. Their name Manx came from the breeding colony on the Isle of Man, since abandoned except for a small colony

171

on the Calf of Man. It was once thought that the shearwaters were the reincarnation of the souls of the dead. Normally silent birds, the throbbing cacophony of their calls as the parents return, in total darkness, to the young in the underground nest burrows terrified superstitious peasants. The calls are part of the identification between parent and offspring and their furtive behaviour is a safety measure – evidence of late arrivals who have been slaughtered by herring gulls and greater black-backed gulls litters the breeding site.

These latecomers arrive from the fishing grounds distended with fish which they have crushed in their crops preparatory to feeding the young, and the gulls wait in the early dawn for them; any shearwater still above ground is quickly despatched.

Shearwaters form only a small part of the seabird population. Auks, razorbills, guillemots and puffins are day-flyers and the cliff ledges ring with their grunts and croaks above the high-pitched call of the kittiwake. But all the sea-going birds, with the notable exception of the herring gull, have declined drastically with the increased frequency of oil spills in the seas around our coastline, and as our dependence on oil increases daily so the seabirds dwindle, killed in the most revolting way.

Other dwellers of the sea, such as seals, are also destroyed by this menace which man seems powerless to contain. Often the worst oil spills seem to occur at the times and places with the greatest concentration of sea creatures. The auks, especially, are totally dependent on rock and cliff face nesting sites; evolution has even given their eggs a distinctive pear-shape so that they will not roll off the ledge as round eggs would do. Auks fill the same ecological niche in the northern oceans as penguins fill in the south, and the similarity in body shape is remarkable; the northern-hemisphere auks have retained the power of flight, however, whereas penguins have lost it.

There was one flightless auk, the great auk, but that was extermi-nated in the last century and we have a special responsibility to make sure that our technological society does not repeat the operation with the great auk's remaining relatives, the razorbill, a small bird bearing a resemblance to its extinct cousin, the little auk, a mere 8 inches long, the guillemot and the clown-like puffin.

Seabirds show perhaps the greatest adaptation to environment of any bird. The gannet, for instance, is protected from concussion on hitting the water during its spectacular fishing dives by a series of air-filled sacs in its shoulders and breast. These absorb the impact as the bird enters the water, allowing it to use its weight to dive quite deep and catch its fish. The other, more common, divers are cormorants and shags, also occupants of the whitewashed breeding ledges. These reptillian-looking birds surprisingly have increased in numbers despite the ever-present menace of oil and depredations by fishermen who say they deprive them of catches.

Cormorants can indeed catch quite large fish, which they swallow whole. Under water they are superb swimmers, often reaching great depths and staying submerged for some minutes at a time. Their plumage is unusual in lacking the waterproofing possessed by most water birds, and consequently they have to dry themselves off in the wind and sun before venturing back into the sea. They are a familiar sight around our coasts, as they stand like heraldic figures with wings outstretched, or like old witches in black bombazine. It is perhaps because of this slightly unreal posed appearance that legends of their being birds of ill luck have been handed down by generations of seamen and turned men's hands against them.

It is not only large black seabirds however that have collected superstitions. The wren has been associated with witchcraft for centuries and there were times in the not too distant past when a wren would be ceremonially sealed up in a hole bored in an apple tree to appease the spirits and bring good crops. Toads, bats and lizards too have shared this doubtful honour of being seen as both bewitched and bewitching creatures. After all, the last trial for witchcraft took place

Wren

less than 200 years ago. There have been only about thirty generations since the Norman conquest in 1066, and superstitions, always widespread in country districts, were easily passed on through the generations.

The village in which I spent my childhood was a remote hamlet with a long recorded history, some of the farms in the area dating back before the time of the Domesday Book. This part of Devon consisted of few families and tightly knit communities, until increased communication and better facilities opened it up to the outside world just before the Second World War. Until that time Bratton Clovelly's only real claim to fame was its appearance in a chronicle by S. Baring Gould called *The Red Spider*. This book, first published in 1887, recorded the daily life of the parish and of one farm in particular, the Saxon homestead of Chimsworthy where a farm has stood for over 1,000 years.

The walls of this farm and of many of the cottages in the village, including the one which my parents owned, were constructed of rubble and wattle-and-daub, a method used for a thousand years before Chimsworthy itself was built. When my father replaced the window in the main room to give us a better view over the moor, he found the walls were over 3 ft thick and as hard as concrete, so hard in fact that the electric percussion hammer burned out. The rubble consisted of pieces of slate dug from the fields, bound together with mud, cow dung and straw. It was evident from the bands of different colours in the wall that the cottage had been built over a period of several years, each layer of mud and rubble being allowed to settle before the next was added.

It had been a worker's cottage and was still very much in the same form as when first built in the fourteenth century. There were signs of the half-floored upper living quarters and additions over the years such as a fireplace at one end of the main lower room. The floor was earth, compacted by the feet of many generations of yeoman-farmer workers. Evidence of their occupation was found by examination of the impacted deposits in the floor. These showed traces of fleas, proving the cottage had been used for housing the small stock as well as the family.

Fleas were still in residence when my family moved in, even though it had not been occupied for some years! The little beasts were

Bratton Clovelly church; it is believed that there has been a place of worship here since Roman times

exceedingly hungry and it took several visits by the health department to rid us of them.

The roof was interesting, the main beam of untrimmed oak being supported at the peak by a fork, also of oak and as hard as iron. The oak had been cut locally, probably from Chimsworthy wood, and had become hardened by time and smoke from the fire. In ancient times the smoke would have found its way into the outside air through a hole in the thatch. This had been replaced in Victorian times with slate, and the rafters supporting the slates were nearly all original, consisting of trimmed oak branches which had been similarly pickled by age and smoke to a wood-worm-free rock-hard texture.

The overall height of the downstairs room, for there was only one, was a little over 6 ft, which, as in so many old cottages, suggests that

Common vetch and white campion

our ancestors were not very tall, a conclusion reinforced by the doorways, none of which was higher than 5 ft 6 in. One feature of the downstairs room, though, defied explanation. In the earth floor running from the front door to the back door was a shallow trench, some 3 in or so deep with smooth sides. It looked as though many feet had worn it down by passing through one door and out of the other. However, as with most things connected with country folk, a perfectly sound reason was soon to come to light. The cottage floor was duly covered with concrete to prevent rising damp, and all the carpets and furniture subsequently placed on top when an unexpected and particularly heavy rainstorm occurred. The water ran down the side of the hill from the school, entered the cottage by the front door and left by the back. The eminent practicality of the trench became obvious! It was a flash-flood drain and it took a lot of hard work and ingenuity to divert the flow.

The people of this village were completely in step with the land they occupied. They had that Celtic look which is still strong in many parts of Devon, small stature and great strength coupled with dark hair and pale skin, a strong genetic type resistant to dilution. My own son exhibits these characteristics, inherited from his Devon mother. A spirit of 'oneness' exhibited itself in the character of the people and it was said you were still a 'Furriner' until your family had lived in the village for several generations.

As with the majority of villages across the land, the hub of social life spun on two spindles, the village pub and the church. The church at Bratton is especially interesting, built on the site of a much earlier religious building, probably Romano-British. The present church of St Mary the Virgin is Norman and inside are several old wall paintings. Churches are generally the repositories of village history and the gravestones and monuments are a rich source of information for the historian. The fact was that the village priest was probably the only truly literate man in the community and consequently the parish records were sometimes the only guideline to local happenings.

Because of its remoteness this part of east Devon seems to have escaped some of the less pleasant aspects of modern farming. For instance Chimsworthy Farm still has the old field system dictated by the production of livestock. The soil is marginal, wet and basically infertile, so to remove hedges for producing cereals would be economically pointless. The old hedgerows contain some of the original hedge species and there is a theory, although it has its detractors, that the number of woody species in a 100-ft length of hedge multiplied by 100

White dead nettle and cocksfoot grass

will give the approximate age of the hedge. By this method of calculation the age of the hedges around Bratton Clovelly averages out at about 600 hundred years, which ties in well with a burst of enclosure of land in Elizabeth I's reign which replaced the old farm system of strip lynchets used all over the hilly areas of the West Country.

As the month of June wanes, the weather begins to settle into a pattern of long warm days and short warm nights, ideal conditions for the growing army of young creatures populating the countryside. Immature grey partridges are now strong on the wing and the pheasant poults fly rather than walk or run when danger threatens. In the fields the clover is flowering and the honey bees bustle from flower to flower in the lazy days of high summer, gathering nectar and pollen to stock their bulging combs which are now ripe for plunder by the bee keeper. Beekeeping was going on at least 3000 years before the Romans invaded our shores; some might say it has been a cult, even a religion. The ancient Britains almost certainly supplemented their diet with honey from the combs of wild colonies of bees which abounded in the wooded, flower-rich countryside.

Bees will often build nests in human habitations, between the gaps in modern cavity walls, so it is likely they colonised primitive huts all those thousands of years ago, which possibly made our unsophisticated ancestors consider the expedient of transferring bee colonies to reed-thatched shelters similar to the type they themselves occupied. Probably the practice of using smoke to quieten the aggressiveness of bees came about in a similar way. It is known that the smoke from primitive man's fire was ducted into the outside air via a hole in the thatch and any bees occupying that thatch would have been pacified by the rising billows.

With the advent of imported cane sugar and later homegrown sugar beet, beekeeping became more of a hobby than a necessity, and during the past 100 years or so was thought rather eccentric; the swarming tendencies of these useful creatures became the subject of many humerous anecdotes. It is only recently that the cult of self-reliance and the growth of so-called health foods has caused beekeeping to become fashionable again and numerous preparations and foods have a honey base. In the past, honey was the only source of sweetening for foods and drinks. Indeed warriors, before donning their woad paint in readiness for battle, would fortify their spirits with liberal draughts of mead, a drink made from honey. Mead production is a logical progression in the practice of apiculture. The washing of pots which contained the raw honey would result in a sugar-and-water mixture which would readily ferment under the influence of natural wild yeasts, and the result of this ferment was mead.

The brew which is sold as mead today is often not the true brew, but contains additions of fruit juices and spices to make it more acceptable. These drinks are actually 'melomel' or 'megethlin', the old name for wines made from honey and fruit. True mead made only from honey and water takes a considerable time for the flavour to mature and lose the raw honey taste modern man finds rather unpalatable, but our ancestors back in the Bronze and Iron ages were not so fussy, and until the widespread brewing of beer came popular in these islands, mead was the generally accepted drink.

Wild bees are uncertain-tempered creatures and domestication has taken away a lot of their sting. Like the bumble bee, the honey bee is an essential constituent of the life of the country; without it there would be only the air currents to blow the life-giving pollen from male flower to female flower, and the only plants growing in our meadows and woodside margins would be grasses.

Bees also have a part to play in the basic petal structure of wild flowers and in the distribution and form of those flowers. Take the foxglove, that sentinel of the woodland floor. The flower has evolved to foil the entry of insects other than the bumble bee, whose fur-covered body is the perfect vehicle for carrying the liberal quantities of pollen hidden at the top of the flower bell. Any creature other than a bumble finds it difficult to pass the barrier of fine hairs which guard the entrance to the foxglove nectary. Even the honey bee has a hard time overcoming this hazard.

By the end of June most foxglove flowers will have been fertilised by the bees and now the plants stand tall and straight in the glades, the bulging green seed cases forcing the dead brown gloves from the fingers of next year's seed.

10
JULY

High summer is at its apogee as July takes the stage. The wild world is becoming accustomed to at least some measure of warmth and light; in the woods the sow badger makes longer hunting expeditions as the cubs are weaned from her milk. She feeds on grubs and worms and any small creatures she can find to build up her depleted store of fat. The cubs can now romp in the glades, trampling the strands of green bracken into the polished earth. The play of young creatures often appears aimless and frolicsome when actually it has a definite purpose, to prepare the cubs for their life in the outside world and the serious business of finding food. Also it establishes individuals in the hierarchy of the community. Badgers are social animals, and a dominance-order in the badger clan is necessary to avoid conflict within the sett.

The sett is the hub of the badger community, constantly being enlarged and improved. Some of them have been occupied by badgers for centuries, the spoil heaps outside the entrance often reaching the proportions of small hills. Usually the badger chooses a site in the side of a bank where the earth strata will allow the largest possible collection of chambers to be constructed with the minimum of effort. This is most clearly shown by examining badger spoil heaps in areas

Badger

where the subsoil is mainly chalk. One of the facts of life known to anyone who farms chalkland is the presence of large numbers of flints, which impede the progress of the plough and damage the cutting edge. By some inbuilt sense the tunnelling badger avoids the substratum which contains the flints, finding for itself a stone-free layer to mine, and in chalky soil setts reach vast proportions, sometimes being hundreds of square feet in area with several entrances and exits.

Badgers are often described as having poor eyesight, and are usually depicted in illustrations for children's books as peering myopically through spectacles perched on the end of their striped noses. In fact their sight is as good as it needs to be in the twilight world they inhabit, where sight is one of the least valuable senses. They are not hunters of large or active prey, their main food consisting of ground-living invertebrates such as worms, small mammals and some carrion. When hunting worms, the best senses to have are those of smell and hearing: and a badger's hearing is very acute. It can detect the slightest sound, and its questing nose, with its large damp surface specially adapted to collect particles of scent from the air, will then attempt to identify it.

Often the badger shares its home, or a disused part of it, with foxes, and contrary to popular opinion there is no animosity between landlord and tenant and little evidence to show that the strong smell of the fox is offensive to the badger. It could be the other way round, for badgers are addicted to taking back to the sett bundles of bedding which contain a considerable proportion of green vegetable matter, including the strong-smelling wild garlic which they collect in arm-fuls, dragging it backwards into the chamber which after a time must begin to smell like the kitchen of an Italian restaurant.

Why they do this is something of a mystery. Possibly it is a disinfectant measure to rid the bedding of parasites, as garlic certainly contains medicinal properties; any self-respecting flea would find such an atmosphere hard to stomach. Although, like all wild creatures, badgers are host to parasites both internal and external, they are exceptionally clean in their toilet habits and dig latrines some distance from their quarters. Evidence that the latrines are being used regularly provides conclusive proof that the sett is occupied.

Because of their secretive habits little was known about the private life of badgers until the early 1930s, when recording the events in their daily life became the practice among a growing band of naturalists and

White bryony

animal-behaviour specialists. Though sometimes one of the most rewarding activities, badger-watching must rank as the least certain in results, as the animals are notoriously wary and the slightest distur-bance will send them rippling back to the sett where they will stay until the observer has left. As well as being uncertain it is indescribably uncomfortable. Cramped muscles ache for movement and the atten-tions of the midges always seem to be at their zenith, striking like so many thousands of red-hot needles, just as the sow comes out to sniff the evening air. Blackbirds 'tic tic' in the stillness and an insomniac robin will sometimes sing his refrain to a silent appreciative wood. It may be imagination, but there always seems to be an air of expectancy preceeding the appearance of the first badger of the evening; a sense of excitement which never palls.

As with all wildlife study there is only one way to do it properly. That is to sit still in a quiet place and watch what is going on. Not only the daily life of the badger will become apparent, all the myriad sounds in the leaf litter can be pinpointed by concentration of the senses: the happenings in the lives of woodmice and the bickering of shrews among the stems of the wood mellick; foxes quietly picking their way, unaware of a human presence so close at hand, sniffing the bluebells which still remain in the more shaded places; damp-eyed deer treading delicately through the curling bracken fronds with infinite care so as not to break the twilight spell.

Predator and prey may co-exist with apparent unconcern within the immediate confines of the predator's home. Often rabbits live in the same warren-cum-sett-cum-earth as badgers and foxes, and they appear to take little or no notice of one another. It is not unusual to see rabbits washing their ears in complete disregard of a fox only feet away who is also having a wash and brush-up before setting out on a hunting expedition.

Badgers appear to take even less notice of rabbits than the foxes do, but this is not hard to understand. As a rule badgers do not catch adult or even half-grown rabbits, though they will dig out a nest which the doe has made for her young. Rabbits do not in fact often have their young ones in the warren. When the time of birth is near the doe takes herself to a quiet place in a nearby field or hedge bottom, and digs a shallow burrow which she lines with fur from her own underside. It is here she deposits her blind babies, resembling pink sausages, leaving them hidden and returning to feed them at regular intervals. It is during the time they are in this temporary nursery that they are at the greatest risk from ground-hunting predators. Even so the rabbit's proverbial breeding success shows that this means of rearing young has much to recommend it.

The fox is almost as adaptable as the rabbit, even though man's hand has always been turned against him, but in more recent years the fashion for fur garments and the high price put upon fox skins has meant that in some areas, especially close to large urban communities, they are shot, snared or trapped in such large numbers that the natural breeding pace is being overtaken. The decline of fox hunting has meant that in some areas where once it would have been considered heresy of the worst sort to shoot or snare a fox, the practice is now accepted as a necessary control. The net result of this is that in inner cities there is a thriving urban fox population with few rabbits, and in the countryside generally the reverse is true. In parts of Devon, Dorset and Cornwall where agriculture is based more on beef, dairy cattle and sheep, and where foxes and buzzards thrive along with a healthy number of stoats, weasels and owls, the problems caused to farmers by rabbits are relatively small.

Fox

July is when the air is full of the largest of our native butterflies. In the oak woods in the New Forest and in Sussex the spectacular purple emperor is on the wing, flying high at the top of the oak trees, only coming to ground to sip water from a puddle or perhaps to land on a dead rabbit or some similar carrion; for beautiful as it is, this insect is

White admiral butterfly (*Ladoga camilla Linn*)

partial to dead meat with a gamey taste. The male's wings are shot with a panel of metallic purple, which is dimly echoed in the female by a mere fine glazing of purple scales on otherwise brown wings. Being a large butterfly, almost half as big again as a peacock, it is a strong flyer and on the rare occasions when it is seen it is usually only briefly as it swoops between the trees.

The New Forest is home to many of the showier butterflies. For instance fritillaries with their russet wings gracefully alight on the heads of thistle, standing tall as lifeguards in a forest ride. With a fluttering, gliding flight the white admiral makes its appearance, to sip nectar from the flowering bramble, jostling for position among the small tortoiseshells, peacocks and ragged-winged commas. There are legions of butterflies at this time of the year, coinciding with a bloom of herbs in the fields. Our forefathers must have looked forward to July, when they could collect more medicinal herbs. Mint, thyme, basil and marjoram were firm favourites, used for the relief of many ills – from whooping cough to providing strengthening baths for weakly children. Cuts and chest ailments appear to have been the main burdens of our ancestors. Many of the herbal remedies were compounded particularly to relieve coughs and bronchitis or to heal wounds. Then came medicines to relieve stomach ailments and last came medicines for ills which were largely incurable or imaginary, plus a few aphrodisiacs and remedies for gout. Herbs must also have been a boon for flavouring meat; in the days before refrigeration it would only keep a short time in the July warmth and probably acquired a strong taste.

The herbs which our forefathers gathered are still appreciated by the army of insects which populate every bank and roadside margin in

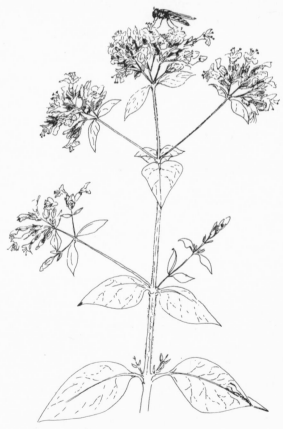

Hoverfly on marjoram

the summer. The rounded flower-head of marjoram is like a magnet to the burnet moths. They push and struggle, fifty to a plant, eager to dip their watch-spring tongues into the nectar, while over the top of their jostling red and black bodies the skipper butterflies hover, looking more like moths than their showy relatives. The burnets do not give way without a struggle. In fact they have few enemies because of their warning black-and-red colouration, which frightens off other food-seekers. Only the young inexperienced bird will grasp a burnet in its beak, for the insect contains a poison which is bitter and acrid and was absorbed by the caterpillar from the food plant.

The war and peace of nature is conducted to strict rules. Signs and signals tell potential aggressors that a creature will fight back or will taste so horrible that it is not worth the effort, but not all keep to the rules. Wasps, for instance, advertise their potential threat to an aggressor by their pattern of black and yellow, so arranged as to warn any adversary that this insect stings; there are insect opportunists who

Honeysuckle

mimic such colours, such as hoverflies and the flies that copy the solitary bees.

A colour-warning pattern is also carried by the adders that bask in the July sun. They are not agressive by nature, but as with the wasp their markings state loud and clear that they can defend themselves if attacked. The pleasing blend of colours on ladybirds, too, is there for a purpose. As well as delighting the human eye it is a warning that they are bad to eat. Nature foresaw the possibilities of chemical warfare millions of years ago and has refined it to perfection.

All the hedgerows and gardens are alive with birdsong and contact calls: nature is overproducing, as she does every year, to ensure that each species will be able to sustain losses yet survive as a species. Any apparent balance in nature is purely accidental. There is a theory that creatures are only the outward manifestation of the genes they carry, each set of genetic material constructing for itself the best vehicle to ensure the gene's survival. It is conjectured that man is alone among the animals on this planet in his ability to reason and to ponder such concepts as immortality, heaven and earth, and his own place upon the earth. The old-style countryman considered that his immortality lay in family continuity, as in the occupation of the same farm or dwelling through the ages by a group of related people.

. All over the country men's occupations are reflected in their sur- names. The frequency of the name Smith obviously stems from the various occupations that used it – ironsmith, silversmith, tinsmith or blacksmith. Many names have a distinctly warlike ring: Fletcher, for instance, is an echo of the times when attaching feathers to arrowshafts· to make the arrow fly true to its target was the task of a craftsman called a fletcher. The arrow itself was fashioned by an arrowsmith and shot from a longbow made of yew by a bowyer.

For others, continuity of employment was imprinted on the indi- vidual not by the acquisition of a surname, but by a pride taken in a particular calling. As a case in point, gamekeepers are often members of the same family, going back from son to father to grandfather and sometimes even great-grandfather. Sadly the carnage of the two world wars abruptly and permanently terminated many of these lines. However, there is a family in Hertfordshire, on the Rothschild Estate, which can proudly boast four generations of gamekeepers. Bernard Double, the present incumbent, took the place of keeper from his father Charles, who in turn took it from his father, and so on. The original Mr Double joined the estate back in the 1880s, in the days when rearing game and duck was a major undertaking. Today the job

Taken in 1890; Charles Edward Double, grandfather to Bernard, is third from left

Taken in 1935 at the luncheon hut, Wilstone, Tring. Grandfather Charles Edward is sixth from left; on his immediate right is his son, Bernard's father, also named Charles Edward

Father and son: Bernard Double and Jeffrey where the luncheon hut once stood

also entails the keepering of a trout-fishing syndicate on one of the reservoirs of the Tring National Nature Reserve – and Mr Double also serves the reserve as a warden, protecting the very birds that his antecedents would have regarded as vermin. Yet the estate still has sporting interests albeit on a limited scale.

Buildings, too, have a continuity, reflecting the purpose for which they were built, sometimes long after they become redundant or fall into disrepair. One had a direct link with the Double family and the estate they serve – a small one-roomed building known as the luncheon hut. It was built so that shooting parties could have somewhere to go for a bite to eat and something to keep out the cold after winter duck-shooting on Wilstone reservoir. Constructed of wood against a brick wall, and with a chimney stack, its roof was a masterpiece of thatching, the peak having a pattern in hazel strips all along the length. The diamond-pane leaded windows let the light into a cedar-panelled room where the guests were served in the days of elegance when each man had his place, be it high or low, in the order of things. Unhappily the luncheon hut became unsafe a few years ago and had to be demolished.

191

Orange tip pupae

The merits of the old order of things are of course debatable; perhaps we are now too far outside the social outlook of those times to be able to judge objectively. However, for the people for whom the estate or farm was the centre of the universe this way of life was. perfectly acceptable. Even though the work was hard and the hours long there was a degree of security and a sense of belonging.

As the luncheon hut ceased to be a centre of lively talk and activity to become a grass-covered mound, so the way of life of the people who used it has slipped away. Now the visitors to this part of the estate are wardens of the National Nature Reserve, the odd passing fisherman out to tempt the large pike for which the lake is justly famous, or the present gamekeeper and his son. Maybe the latter will grow up to inherit his father's post and so become the fifth keeper in the family.

With the coming of the long days of high summer wild creatures can enjoy a security and indolence afforded to them by the heavy growth of rank herbage. Caterpillars, which have been growing apace since their hatching in the early spring, are full-grown and wander in search of a place to pupate and reorganise their cells into a new winged state within the safety of their chrysalis. For some this winged state will never be, for they carry inside their bodies the living larvae of ichneumon wasps. Having feasted on the growing caterpillar, these are now ready to emerge from the living tissue of the unfortunate insect.

This is nature's way, even though it seems cruel. It ensures there will not be too many individuals of any creature for long. The ichneumon wasps in their turn, when they hatch from their yellow silken pupal cases grouped around the dried skin of their dead host, will fall prey to zebra-striped jumping spiders. These tiny insects are the cats of the spider world. They have incredible eightfold eyesight and their amazing reactions enable them to stalk a fly, leaping the final inch to catch it before it has time to become airborne.

July is a good month for spiders, from the tiny mimics who hide within flowers to snare visiting insects, to the stalking wolf spiders of the grasslands and meadows who run down their unfortunate victims with a burst of speed.

Many people find spiders unlovely and I must admit to being an arachnophobe (someone with an irrational fear of spiders). This was not always the case – as with all phobias a specific event triggered off the response. My fear of spiders came at a time when I was involved in the ripening and marketing of bananas for a major importer. For ease

Spider

of shipment bananas are exported from the growers in a green state, then ripened here in heated rooms until ready for the consumer. The bananas remain on the stalks sealed in plastic tubes, and dormant within these tubes, among the fruit, are a variety of creatures, depending on the country of origin of the crop. The importers concerned here received the majority of their supplies from the Dutch Cameroons and the shipments were always checked on unloading as they often contained snakes, some of which were somewhat venomous when warmed to activity in the ripening chambers.

On one particular occasion there had been no snakes in the cargo, and the fruit was placed to ripen, after which it was cut from the stalks with a curved knife and boxed for transport to the retail outlets. I was daydreaming about the sunshine outside and slicing off the hands of bananas with little thought for the job in hand when, on slicing a rather big hand and turning it over to inspect the underside, a large and exceedingly hairy spider appeared. It stared at me with all of its eight shiny black eyes. I was transfixed with an irrational fear which paralysed thought and muscle and stood stock still for several seconds. In the end the spider moved first, walking deliberately toward my thumb which still gripped the cut-off stalk.

Whether I threw the hand of yellow fruit from me, or whether I simply dropped it I know not. But it landed on the floor equidistant between me and the wall of the ripening room. Until that time I was not aware that these large so-called 'bird-eating' spiders could jump, but as the bananas hit the floor so the spider leapt from the fruit and landed on the wall some 4 ft from the ground. Had it decided to bound toward me I would have been a hospital case from sheer shock.

The local zoo was summoned and the spider captured by a breezy young man with a small butterfly net. He put it in a bottle, still very much alive, and met my enquiry as to how poisonous it was with a reassuring reply. 'Oh not very, but it was a good job you never put your hand on it. The fangs tend to tear the skin rather.' Leaving me white and shaking he carried away his prize to the zoo.

This encounter and subsequent nightmares about spiders left a deep impression and even now a harmless spider in the bath makes me go cold. It is little consolation to know that I am one among a multitude when it comes to phobias about wild creatures. One of the most 'popular' phobias, if that is not an unfortunate choice of word, is against snakes. Snakes induce shivers and cold sweats in the most unlikely people and their fear is perhaps slightly more rational, for the adder really is poisonous.

Snakes are fascinating reptiles which have reached the heights of adaptation, and literally can walk across the surface of the earth on the tips of their ribs. There are three species of snake in this country: the adder, or viper, the smooth snake and the grass snake.

The grass snake is the most widely distributed of the three, being found in nearly every county on the mainland, although absent from Ireland and northern Scotland. They reach considerable lengths and large females have been recorded up to 6 ft long, but they are non-poisonous, living on frogs and small mammals which they swallow whole. They swim well and are often found near water where their prey is abundant.

The adder, on the other hand, is a creature of dry places and likes a heath and heather environment. It can often be seen in the south basking on dry banks in the sunshine. Despite their reputation they are not aggressive and if disturbed will slide away to cover; but if trodden on they will bite in self-defence, and the bites are serious. Only a few deaths from adder bites are recorded, but unfortunately those most vulnerable are children or the elderly. Adders prey mainly on mice and will even tackle a weasel, which must present quite a fight; the speed of the adder's strike is so fast the human eye cannot follow the movement.

The other British species, the smooth snake, is rare now and confined to the dry heathland of Dorset, Hampshire and the adjoining counties. It preys on sand lizards and small mammals, which it captures by coiling tightly around them until they are sufficiently subdued to be swallowed whole. A snake's jaw is unusual in that it can be disjointed to allow large prey to be swallowed, and because all snakes lack breastbones or shoulder joints the ribs are floating, which allows for accommodation of a large meal in the body cavity without distress to the snake.

Of the three, only the adder has young born without a protecting eggshell, the eggs being carried inside the mother snake until ready to be born, hatching inside her and the young snakes appearing in the outside world all ready to move and take their place in the scheme of things. The smooth snake and the grass snake produce eggs which hatch soon after laying. Snakes have become less common in recent years. The grass snake especially has suffered from loss of habitat, and the draining of ponds and ditches with consequently fewer of the frogs which form the bulk of their diet.

One animal which is often thought to be a snake is the slow-worm, which is actually a legless lizard. These reptiles have the ability of

Corncrake

many lizards to shed their tails when they are handled or caught by the tail. This is a useful ruse as the predator is fooled into thinking that the wriggling tail is the complete animal and the slow-worm is able to glide away to grow another tail.

The corn and barley in the fields are reaching maturity and the inhabitants are busying themselves in the miniature forest of stems unaware of the catastrophe of the harvest to come. Stoats stalk the rows like tigers in an Indian bamboo jungle, catching unwary voles who nibble blunt-nosed into the springing wheat. At night, barn owls hover like enormous white moths over the waving ranks of stalks waiting to pounce on any unwary animal that ventures out into the open, while cockchafers with antennae resembling toothbrushes whizz heavily across the fields in the manner of unguided missiles.

The loss of the corncrake from all but a very few counties has meant there are not many creatures left actually associated with cornfields. One of them, however, is the mouse first identified by the Selborne vicar, Gilbert White; the harvest mouse, fairy of the cornfield – so small it can climb a cornstalk.

These animals are commoner than at first appears, for although they are associated with cornfields they are also dwellers of the field margins, and their beautiful intricate ball-shaped nests are most often built in the tall grasses at the field's edge, rarely in the open field. Their fur is a shade of reddish-gold, the young harvest mice being greyer than their parents. As acrobats they have few equals and swing and scramble through the stalks of the crop, holding on with their prehensile tails, reaching out with tiny, almost human, hands for the next secure hold. Their numbers fluctuate wildly and they are greatly affected by the weather. Cold, wet springs will devastate the population, whereas a mild dry spring and warm summer will produce too many of them.

Harvest mouse

The short-tailed field vole is also a ready victim of unfavourable conditions. Probably the most numerous of the small mammals in this country it is the little animal on which most of the predatory birds and animals depend. In good years the voles provide a veritable bonanza for kestrels, owls, weasels and foxes, and the field margins and banks are alive with their furry bodies scurrying to and fro. Normally they are peaceable animals, but during these periodic surges of population they become irritable and fight among themselves. This is probably a tendency protective to the species, limiting contact and further breeding until finally there is an outbreak of disease and the numbers subside to normal levels. As with the Scandinavian lemming, which has similar dramatic increases in numbers, the bank vole and field vole seem little affected by man. Although feral cats and tame house cats wreak havoc on a small local scale, voles overall have benefited from man's intervention. Such unlovely innovations as the motorways have provided havens for furry beings, and their undisturbed banks teem with small mammals of all sorts.

Bank vole

Because the banks need to be stable and not liable to landslip, quite a number of our major roads and motorways in particular are allowed to remain unsprayed by weedkillers, so the herbage grows thick and uncontrolled, to the delight of such inhabitants. The strong root growth of the wild plants holds the newly heaped soil together. The majority of motorway banks are now well established, and many species of plants thrive within sight and sound of the thundering stream of lorries and cars which provides a constant movement of air, helping the grasses to be fertilised. On this profusion of plant life lives a host of insects, birds and mammals, prey and predator.

The kestrel has become the bird of the motorway and can always be seen hanging on the wind over the traffic. Even the woodland-dwelling sparrowhawk flies around the motorway shrubbery waiting its chance, and owls too, the short-eared as well as the barn owl and tawny, float over the motorway banks. The day-flying predators seem to suffer only a low mortality rate from the traffic, but owls are not so fortunate. They are killed in large numbers, probably dazzled by headlights which induce a temporary blindness similar to that caused in humans by bright photographic flash bulbs; in the period of disorientation brought on by the glare the owl flies into a vehicle.

The little owl also finds good pickings in the lush growth of motorway banks, as it is mainly insectivorous in its diet and has the advantage of being a daytime as well as night-time predator. In the 1950s the little owl became very common, spreading out from its point of introduction – it is not a native bird. As with many introduced species it found an empty niche in nature and colonised it. It spread quickly, but earned an unjustified reputation as a killer of game chicks and songbirds, whereas its diet is mainly composed of beetles, worms and other large invertebrates.

The advent of chemical insecticides had a swift and devastating effect on this bird and within five years or so it almost disappeared, reaching the status of a rarity. However, the past few years have seen its re-emergence on the British scene and, as with the kestrel, the motorway has been its saviour.

The little owl nests in holes in dead trees and the loss of millions of elms through Dutch elm disease has meant there are fewer breeding sites available. But it will nest in buildings and has been known to use nest boxes put up for tawny owls. It has a peculiarity all of its own, that of standing on a branch or the top of a post and bobbing and weaving from side to side. The observer is left with the impression that the bird's eyesight is poor and it is trying to focus on possible prey. This, of course, is an illusion. In common with other members of the owl clan its eyesight is superb and the bobbing and weaving is a method used to assess range accurately.

Little owl

Scottish wild cat

This century has seen the establishment in the English countryside of various animal and plant introductions. Man has often tried, with bizarre results, to enrich his life. Some plants, such as the introduced conifers, have had little effect on the environment, unless like the spruce they have been planted in great numbers as in Forestry Commission plantations, where large areas have been given over to the growth of softwoods, sometimes to the detriment of the native flora and fauna. The dense cover of conifer plantations has, however, actually given a chance of survival to some creatures who would otherwise have joined the ranks of extinct British and Scottish wildlife.

Chief among these has been the Scottish wild cat, which although looking rather like a yellowish version of the domestic tabby shares few of its endearing traits, and is reputed to be untameable. Close inspection of this 'tiger of the pines' reveals the difference between the two. The wild cat has a true hunter's litheness and grace which puts most domestic cats in the shade. Usually the only view to be had of it is when it is taken by surprise, caught on the defensive with its yellow and grey fur on end, ears flattened and lips drawn back menacingly. In repose, or following its normal life, the cat carries its ears pricked and alert for every sound, although not as erect as the ears of a domestic cat. A wild cat's ears form a shallow V on top of its head. Its legs are longer and slimmer, its body is also longer with the head carried

200

lower. The tail is full and ringed with black, with a blunt-ended black tip.

As with their domestic cousin, the toms are solitary and only visit the female when they are ready to mate, which they do with much caterwauling and screaming. When the kittens are born they are blind and helpless and look like large bumble-bees with black, yellow and grey striped fur. The she-cat talks to them continuously in a series of low chirrups and if she is disturbed she communicates her discomfort to the kittens even before their eyes are open, and they will hiss and spit although quite unaware of what is threatening them.

The wild cat has spread out from its stronghold in Sutherland and the Highlands; up to now it has been seen as far south as Yorkshire. It is unlikely to return to the main counties of England, partly because of the lack of wild habitat and partly because it would interbreed with domestic cats, thereby diluting the purity of the breed. Also it is not resistant to the domestic cat's diseases and quickly succumbs to feline enteritis and the like.

It is a formidable hunting machine, having all the attributes in full measure: perfect binocular vision, sharp teeth and claws and the strength, tenacity and courage to tackle almost any prey, even young deer. Because of this it has been ruthlessly destroyed for attacking grouse and pheasant. Actually its main food is the mountain blue hare or the rabbit. It would never cause severe depredations on stocks because, as with all successful predators, it hunts over a large territory.

11

AUGUST

The last of the summer months lies upon the land. Sometimes sultry, often thundery, August shimmers on to the harvest. The farming community pray to gods old and new for a period of continuous dry weather to ripen the grain crowding the ears of the crop. Waving fields of corn are streaked blonde and green, here and there dotted with poppies like spots of blood.

The seed-eating birds are having – literally – a field day. Goldfinches flit and hover over the meadows picking the gleanings of the grass seed, which falls from the ripe brome like rain to the ground beneath. On the hedge banks clusters of marjoram are topped with a brown umbrella as the flowers die and the seed cases ripen. Green-veined-white butterflies flutter like snowflakes over the drying grasses and the countryside takes on its raiment of gold.

In the southern half of the country the predominant August colour is softly amber, but in the north and in Scotland the colour tinging the hills is of a royal hue as the heather comes into full flower. Upland bees buzz around gathering the champagne of the crop; heather honey has long been famous for its unique subtle flavour.

The young grouse are now strong on the wing which will stand them in good stead for the 'glorious twelfth' and the visiting guns who will shatter the peace of the moors with the crack of shotgun fire as the beaters advance across the spiky turf between the woody stems of the heather, driving the birds before them. Grouse present a difficult target. Using the wind and the terrain to their advantage they speed like cannonballs, hugging the contours of the moor. It is conjectured that without organised grouse shooting the bird itself would have become extinct by now, but this is an over-simplification. Grouse feed on heather shoots which grouse-moor keepers encourage by strip burning of moorland. During the late nineteenth and early twentieth centuries, the heyday of grouse shooting, over-burning damaged the habitat, leaving less moorland for the grouse. They can thrive without man's protection and because their numbers are fewer, disease is less of a problem. In the wild state, not managed by man, the main enemy of the hardy grouse is wet weather in spring which kills many chicks.

Grouse, as we know them, are a relic of the time when Britain was returning to warmth after the last Ice Age and the red grouse, which is peculiar to these islands, was isolated from the continental Arctic race now found in Scandinavia and the steppes of Russia. The willow grouse of Norway, to which the red grouse is closely related, is not dependent on heather and ling, but dependent or not the red grouse has survived for at least 10,000 years on the northern moorlands of Scotland and has extended its range to the north Yorkshire moors. There are also introduced colonies on Dartmoor and Exmoor.

Another Ice Age relic of the high tops is the ptarmigan, a bird

Red grouse

203

similar to the red grouse but smaller and having the ability to change its plumage to white in the winter. The ptarmigan is a bird of mountain places and needs winter camouflage to protect itself against the depredations of its natural predator the golden eagle. Ptarmigan are found only on the higher areas of the Scottish mountains and are rarely seen below 2,000 ft. Due to lack of human interference in such regions they are, unlike their cousin the grouse, trusting of man. Hill walkers or mountaineers can often get quite close to them before they whirr off uttering their croaking calls, disappearing into the mist like ghosts. The grouse family generally is well adapted to its harsh environment and even the lowland member of the family, the black-cock, has young which can fly at an astonishingly early age. Young ptarmigan fly at only ten days, young blackcock at two weeks.

The eagle chicks have tried their wings by August and have left the wild and lonely eyrie built of sticks on a high crag. They test their power and mastery over the elements with increasingly long soaring flights and clumsy stoops at young hares. These initial sorties are not very efficient as a means of finding food so it is just as well that the parent birds still bring them choice morsels, but they are vital practice against the time when they will hunt on their own.

The raven is another bird of the mountainous north but more adaptable than the eagle and more widely distributed over the rest of the country, though still a bird of wild places. This was not always so. In the time of Elizabeth I they lived around London and scavenged the streets for scraps and refuse. Now they share their Welsh fastness with another ex-urbanite the red kite, once also common in the city. Shakespeare actually warned the washerwomen to guard their clothes drying on the line from the red kites who would take them to build nests in church towers. Sadly the kites are now rare and confined to the hills of Wales and occasionally Devon, along the edge of the moor.

In the woodlands bordering the moor buzzards rear their young to soar above the granite tors, remanants of the plugs or centres of long-extinct volcanoes. Time and the elements have weathered the cones until only the hardest granite pieces are left sticking out from the skyline like strange sculptures. On the inner moor, where it is bleak and lonely, far from places where summer tourists flock to feed the ponies, the tiny merlin, smallest of the native breeding falcons, chases meadow pipits across the gorse-covered hillsides. Merlins are unusual among falcons in that they are ground-nesters, usually rearing their young at the base of a gorse bush. They are about the same size as a mistle-thrush and masterful fliers, as are all falcons, rarely failing to

Merlin chasing meadow pipit

bring down their quarry. The Dartmoor population migrates in the winter to the continent of Europe, but the merlins of the north are resident. Even in the gentler climate of the south the moorland environment imposes severe restrictions on the types and numbers of animals, plants and insects which can inhabit it.

Dartmoor has been drastically altered by man over the centuries. Most of the outer area of the moor and its valley slopes were wooded, clothed with dense oak forests, but the demands of industry for charcoal to smelt ores for tin, copper, silver and even gold required that the oak woods be stripped from the landscape, leaving only relics of the Dartmoor forests. Although the forests have gone much evidence of the ancient mines and mining communities still exists and towns like Tavistock and Ashburton were 'stannary towns' where mined minerals were taken for refining and assaying. This left a legacy of metal-working skills which died only recently.

The smiths of the West Country were skilled in fashioning the iron tools essential for farming in this fertile but hilly country. The bagging hook and the sickle were developed to high perfection. In fact the forge at the Devon village of Sticklepath, now open to visitors as a museum, produced hand-forged and hand-ground farming and gardening tools until 1960.

The design of tools for gardening, farming, forestry or woodworking has been progressing ever since our cave-dwelling ancestors chipped a flint for a cutting edge, but until this century wood was the main construction material and the fertile minds of the country craftsmen devised a vast array of tools to deal with it. The majority of our native trees yield wood which is hard compared with conifer and difficult to work. In consequence saws that could tackle hard woods effectively without totally exhausting the sawyer were needed. Before the advent of the steam saw during Victoria's reign, the 'pit saw' was used to produce planks of equal width, and the skill of the sawyer was incredible considering the saw was a monster 10 ft long with an upright handle at each end. This handle was drawn backwards and forwards, up and down, by the efforts of two men: one of them worked in a pit below the log, pulling the saw downwards through the wood, while the other stood above and pulled the saw blade upwards.

In spite of the hardness of the work, which went on in all weathers, the planks cut by this method were generally true to thickness along their length, which could be as much as 15 ft. The mind boggles at the thought of sawing a 15 ft oak tree into planks 2 in thick with a hand tool, but to the early Victorian craftsmen pit saws were part of the natural scheme of things, as unavoidable as the August thunderstorms which flattened the ripening corn. The timber they produced was fashioned into all manner of things required for daily life. In a relatively simple society wood has certain advantages: it can be worked cold and a carpenter's shop can be set up temporarily in a barn or cowshed which then reverts to its original use.

Certain crafts combine the skills of the carpenter and joiner with those of the blacksmith. The building of carts for farm work and transport is a prime example. Most carts, waggons and carriages up till the sixteenth century had solid wooden wheels, for iron was not in everyday local use. Another factor influenced the design of the cart and with it the wheel. While solid wheels held sway the speed of transport was limited by the weight of the structure, which made it necessary to use oxen as the main draught animals and although they are immensely powerful they are also very slow.

The timber famine brought about by charcoal burning for iron-working to some degree dictated the design of lighter wheels with wooden rims and spokes shod with iron tyres to resist wear. These new wheels were not only more economical of materials than the solid wheels but also combined the virtues of lightness and strength with an accurate circumference, allowing carts to be lighter also. Another advantage was that these less cumbersome waggons could be pulled by animals much faster than the plodding oxen.

At least until Elizabethan times, the dense woodland covering the country made road-building and moving about in general slow and difficult, the main routes still being those built by the Romans 1,000 years previously. But as woodland was cut down for the needs of farming, and the population became more affluent and wider-ranging, so faster travel was becoming both necessary and possible. The horse, with its superior speed but lesser strength, again became supreme. Lighter carts and spoked wheels became not only desirable but an absolute necessity.

Until Elizabethan times the heavy horse was deemed unsuitable for use on the land. It was an instrument of war, and as such the province of the nobility. It was the tank of its day; the British war horse was famous throughout the old world. With its body armour and mounted steel-clad knight it presented a formidable sight and sound bearing down on ill-equipped foot soliders. Well over a ton of flesh and steel is not a foe to stand and face with only a spear and shield. However, the English longbow and the bodkin-pointed arrow it fired revolutionised warfare. The longbow, made of English yew, could put an arrow through the strongest armour deep enough to mortally wound man or horse, and so began the decline of the war horse. But the great horses with their strength and placid willing dispositions were easily converted to service on the land. With the more settled domestic scene, as barons and landowners gave up the age-old practice of feuding with one another, and turned their energies to building up their estates, the draught horse in fact became infinitely valuable.

Larger tracts of land could now be ploughed in a shorter time than was formerly possible and in consequence of this efficiency landowners began to look longingly at the strips farmed by their tenants and serfs. It was not long before these strips were annexed and brought under the plough. The dominance of the heavy horse was not to be called into question until the age of steam and the coming of the tractor. Like the sheep, the horse has played a big part in shaping the land and indeed still has some influence upon it. The network of roads and byways is a monument to droving tradition and the pack horses which plied the wares of a simple economy throughout the length and breadth of England, Scotland and Wales.

Fox hunting has long been a popular sport with people ranging from stockbrokers to farmers, and was in its heyday in the eighteenth and nineteenth centuries. Foxes need cover, horses need good fences and stout hedges over which to test their skill, and the riders like an interesting landscape through which to ride in pursuit of the fox. The big landowners of the past had the money and the influence to get what they wanted and we still enjoy the landscape bequeathed to us by these environmentally untutored people. They gave us the pattern of fields and coverts, rides and paths, much of which remains.

With modern affluence more people are taking to riding for pleasure and the horse has again come into favour. These riders are very much aware of today's changing environment and vocal in their protests. The crafts connected with horse riding have of necessity revived too. Saddlery, the working of fine leather, farriery and the attendant skills of the blacksmith, are all in demand, as are special clothes and all that horsey paraphernalia with which the initiated surround themselves.

One small point that may contribute to the horse's popularity over the next few decades is the fact that it runs on non-fossil fuel, is self-reproducing, gives its rider healthy exercise and is good for the garden; what car can claim all that?

I mentioned in a previous chapter that sheep-grazed land is extremely valuable as habitat for a variety of plants and insects, most of which have become reduced in numbers over the past twenty years or so. Of the plants, orchids have most markedly declined, of the insects the chalkhill blue. This downland butterfly is the jewel of August: a gorgeous iridescent blue, it flits over the drying grasses looking for a mate, and the female perches on the grass with her brown wings closed showing the spotted underside. The disparity in the markings on individual butterflies makes the chalkhill blue fascinating

Chalkhill blue on horseshoe vetch

from an entomologist's point of view. Such are the variations that two entomologists have written a book completely devoted to aberrations from the norm: *A Monograph of the British Aberrations of the Chalk-Hill Blue Butterfly*, by P. M. Bright and H. A. Leeds, makes compulsive reading.

The food plant of the chalkhill blue caterpillars is horseshoe vetch, a low-growing member of the pea family. In the latter stages of development they even take on a yellow hue to match the vetch flowers. Unfortunately the butterfly was heavily collected in the latter part of the nineteenth century, so much so that its numbers became seriously depleted, especially in the Hertfordshire area where Victorian collctors used to stay in local hostelries awaiting the emergence of the first silver-blue butterfly. Competition for unusual specimens was fierce and there are tales of considerable sums of money changing hands on the field when a particularly choice specimen fell to the net. Happily this type of collecting is a thing of the past and depredation by collectors is minute in proportion to natural mortality from birds, spiders and the weather.

Collecting butterflies or moths was probably one of the most important factors to influence the thinking of naturalists in the late nineteenth century. For many of them it was the first tangible proof of the concept of evolution in action, even though the idea had been propagated many years earlier by Charles Darwin, himself no mean entomologist. Many children have embarked upon a lifelong interest in the study of the natural world by the chance capture of a butterfly or moth, or the collecting and subsequent identification of a caterpillar. I fall into this category myself. As a child in Cornwall my interest in the natural world lacked direction, I simply soaked up information and observations like a sponge. Near my home, above the Gannel estuary, stood Trenance Gardens, an area of woodland growing on the steep slopes of the upper end of the estuary. The woods were rich in butterflies and moths, many of which, like the high brown and silver-washed fritillaries, were too fast-flying for easy capture. The wall brown and speckled wood were easier, and soon a sizeable collection was pinned into shoe boxes on a layer of cork. Early one summer morning I escaped from the pre-breakfast flurry and took my dog Tarzan for a walk. Tarzan was an excellent name for him: he was a greyhound bred by my father but had continued to grow until he was too large for racing, being at least 4 in taller than average and heavily built. His large size and my rather small stature turned a walk into a series of dashes from tree to tree and other marking posts with me

White admiral pupa

hanging on to the lead and offering little resistance to the inevitable progress. However, on this particular morning the punctuated dashes were rather more leisurely than usual, and I had time to look around and so spotted something interesting.

One of the street lamps stood against a close-boarded fence at the entrance to the gardens, and the light the previous evening had attracted quite a few moths; some of them were still there, clinging to the weathered surface of the fence. The only way to stop Tarzan's progress was to tie him to a lamp-post. This I did, then examined the visitors on the fence. To a child's eye the whole collection was exotic: lime hawk moths, eyed hawks and, best of all, several furry-bodied, orange and white winged garden-tiger moths. Despair and ecstasy mingled within me. On the one hand I had found them, yet on the other hand I had nothing in which to put them. They might all fly away never to be seen again. Taking courage in both hands and the dog lead in one, I hurtled homewards, actually managing to get ahead of the dashing dog who regarded it all as a tremendous game. I arrived home too breathless to speak and flew about in a panic looking for a suitable container. My mother, who was used to my collecting things, took no notice. (She rarely intervened unless I was about to make off with an irreplaceable kilner jar or the box my father kept his stiff collars in.) One of the ever-present shoe boxes came to hand. How and why we always had shoe boxes is beyond my comprehension, for at that time there were only four of us in the family and none of us had more than two feet each. Still out of breath I ran back frantically to the moths. They were still there, oblivious of their fate. Almost in tears with relief I put them in the box and carried them home triumphantly.

My mother was unimpressed; she didn't care too much for moths. My father was busy feeding fourteen greyhound puppies who lived in a compound at the end of the large unkempt garden. The greyhounds were the product of his own kennels, called 'Torvene', and with this illustrious-sounding name he hoped to become the winner of the'Greyhound Derby'. Although the Derby eluded him the dogs he bred did have some success. My elder brother had also seen me coming and beat a hasty retreat. So I went off to school without any breakfast, which I was too excited to eat anyway, to share my discovery with a few selected friends.

Death's head hawk moth

For the rest of that summer I visited the moth fence regularly and was rarely disappointed. What attracted the moths to that particular lamp and no other in the road remained a mystery but gradually my collection grew until it was the envy of all my friends, who although allowed to view the collection were not told from whence it came.

211

I still examine fences beside lamps, hoping to find a moth mine. Even though I no longer collect them they are infinitely fascinating.

Mid-August sees the young swifts and swallows on the wing, and family parties hawk for flies over the thunderstorm-ruffled surface of ponds and streams; large dragonflies hover in forward and reverse flight, snapping up insects in the sultry air. The cuckoos, now silent, prepare for the long migration which will take them back to Africa for another year. Their young, reared by wren, meadow pipit, reed warbler and other such birds, are competing with their true parents for the hairy caterpillar which shuffles along like a clothes-brush over the dusty earth.

Spotted flycatcher

With the fledging of young birds and the breaking up of breeding pairs, the males no longer defend and proclaim the territories of the past nesting season; even the dawn chorus, so delightful a feature of the spring and summer, is subdued. Late nesters like the spotted flycatcher still have broods squeaking in ivy-clad nests, often built on the side of an old tree. The adult birds, sleek in their brown and grey flecked plumage, flit and swoop to catch passing insects.

Armies of ants form up their aerial battalions as winged males and future queens hatch from pupae in the darkness of underground nests. They struggle up to the sunlight to take part in the greatest, indeed the only, flying contest of their lives, when the new queens and their consorts take to the air in millions to mate. The males die, but the newly fertile queens land and become wingless for the rest of their lives. The annual bonanza of flying ants drives the birds into a frenzy of feeding. Sparrows, starlings and even gulls join the consummately skilled swallows, swifts and martins in the scramble, and so huge are the ant swarms they look like rising smoke in the distance.

Being communal insects, ants and bees are of constant interest to the human race and there are many references in literature to the similarities between these insects and human society. To the casual observer the parallels seem strong enough, but in fact the functioning of an ant colony is more similar to that of one of man's modern inventions, the computer. Each ant acts as part of a circuit rather than as an individual. Computers make decisions on the 'and–or' principle, but alone the worker ants have no motivation. It is only as part of a great mass serving the queen that they have any function at all. Even the paths to and from the ant colony are like the wires of a computer, containing signals. These are carried by ferramones, which are a subtle combination of smells used to guide members of the colony to the centre.

Ants do not have intelligence to help them or the power of reasoning. Without the queen the colony lacks direction, and because worker ants are infertile the colony would soon cease to exist.

Bees, on the other hand, are a little more autonomous. Nevertheless they are mainly automatic in their responses to the outside world. They have a built-in clock and a set of magnets in their bodies which allow them to navigate with remarkable accuracy. The worker bees, which are infertile females like the worker ants, spend some time in the nest after they hatch from the pupae, and go through a period of apprenticeship, learning the ways of the hive, its orientation in relation to the magnetic pole and the signals which other workers employ to guide the colony to a source of nectar. This period of learning is limited to three or four weeks, during which the apprentice bees busy themselves cleaning the comb and the surrounds of the hive, fanning the air to keep the temperature even and attending to the needs of the queen. The learning is slight, merely an adaptation of a set of pre-conditioned responses to the conditions of a particular hive.

The famous dance of the bees, when a returning worker indicates to her sisters the direction and distance of a source of food, is remarkable and demonstrates the existence of the bee's clock and its magnetic orientation: the dance alters during the day in relation to the sun's position in the sky.

Many other animals have the ability to align themselves with the earth's magnetic force, and recently evidence has been discovered of a magnet composed of tiny crystals of a material called magnetite, a naturally occurring mineral. It is thought that in the eye-socket of a homing pigeon this material, and the nerve-endings which terminate in its vicinity, assist the birds to navigate in relation to their surroundings even when the sun or moon is obscured by cloud. There is little doubt that other birds which undertake long and accurate migrations will also be found to have some of this material in their skulls.

Why the pigeon should have such an extremely well-developed homing instinct is still unclear. The bird from which it is descended is the cliff-face-dwelling rock dove, a singularly sedentary bird which has been domesticated by man for many hundreds of years. In its native surroundings it does not undertake long journeys and seems only to be stirred into action when a passing predator, such as a peregrine falcon, threatens its security. The rock dove was not tamed for the purpose of sending messages. It was bred purely for the benefit of the fresh meat produced by the young pigeons or squabs. Dovecotes were very much part of the architecture of the country house; even the peasant had his dovecote on a pole. And, as the Industrial Revolution brought farm workers from the land into towns they wanted to take with them such of their livestock as they could accommodate; the easiest would have been chickens and, of course, the free-flying pigeon. As time passed and the ex-farm worker became more urbanised, the practice of killing pigeons for food probably grew less popular. Industrial workers were also more mobile, and if a man moved from one town to another taking his pigeons with him, he would have discovered their homing instinct; some of the birds would almost certainly have tried to return to their former homes.

Once this trait was confirmed the instinct was selectively bred. Man has always selected and bred in his animals or birds any traits that make them more useful. When pigeons became more valued for homing ability than for food, then the urge to compete with other pigeon owners demanded further selection – of birds that possessed not only a sure homing ability but also the necessary speed to be first to return to the loft.

Many small domesticated animals now kept as pets were kept for more practical purposes before the industrial revolution. Rabbits, for instance, were farmed in the wild in warrens. These were enclosures where rabbits could burrow into a bank and multiply in a natural environment, being harvested for meat and skins by the 'warreners'. But urban dwellers did not have large areas of land for rabbit produc-

Old English rabbit, arguably the most attractive of the fancy rabbit breeds

tion, so began to keep them in hutches. Here again the spirit of competition soon produced larger animals for more meat, or colourful variations attractive for their fur and markings.

The 'English' rabbit is one of these and arguably the most attractive of the domestic breeds. Its facial markings are similar to those of a panda and its body is pure white with a long elegant black line running the length of the back and black spots on its sides. It soon became a favourite and has remained so. There are a number of alternative colour combinations, official 'standards' have been set and the aim is to produce ever more perfect animals to win at agricultural and rabbit-society shows all over the country.

The ways in which man has adapted animals to his benefit are legion. The many varieties of fowls are examples – from the egg-laying machines that live out their lives in battery houses to the elegant fighting cocks whose long legs used to be adorned with vicious 3-in spikes. In the days when the sport of cock fighting was legal they were 'set' to tear an opponent to shreds. There are several types of fighting cock. The commonest and also the most attractive are the bantams,

Bantam game cock – lord of the rickyard

miniature versions of domestic poultry closely resembling the original jungle fowl in size and form. Bantams vary tremendously in shape and plumage and it was usual to allow them the free run of the yard and fields whilst keeping the egg-laying breeds, such as Rhode Island Reds, in enclosures. Bantams were not usually used for meat or egg production.

Breeding these birds has become fashionable again and many rare and attractive varieties are coming back into their own. One of the prettiest is the 'silky' – an unlikely creature whose plumage resembles fur, because the feather veins lack the 'hook and eye' structure of the normal feather.

The increasing interest in the rarer poultry breeds is part of the upsurge of interest generally in our past and in the animals developed in specific districts isolated by our forefathers' lack of mobility. Many of these types, although not in themselves perfect farm animals, had certain characteristics which make it desirable to preserve some of them as a reservoir of useful animal genes for the future. Sadly some have slipped away into the history books, but even here attempts have been made, with some success, to reintroduce certain features by selective breeding. The Norfolk horn sheep is a case in point. The last of the pure animals died out in the early 1970s but a back breeding programme has successfully re-established certain of their qualities in the new Norfolk horn. Other rare sheep have also become a commercial success. The thick-fleeced Dorset horn with their very early twin lambs are exported all over the world to inject their desirable features into other flocks.

Enthusiasts for preserving the abandoned breeds were looked on as eccentrics until quite recently, but the practice is now recognised as being of real benefit to the farming community as a whole. Even old plant species, used in the past for crops and now preserved only as relics, have a value as genetic material. Some of the older types of cereals, although too long in the straw for modern mechanised harvesting, have a sturdy resistance to plant diseases which can

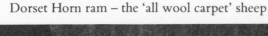

Dorset Horn ram – the 'all wool carpet' sheep

sometimes be grafted on to their short-strawed high-yielding relatives by genetic engineers in the plant-breeding institutes. The supply of petrochemical-based pest-control products is finite, and when exhausted vulnerable crop plants may be left unprotected. It must be better to grow crops which have their own resistance, where possible, rather than relying on costly protection from a can.

Several interesting experiments have been carried out on the back breeding of plants and animals to discover what species were in vogue during the Iron Age, and among other things the specialists have come up with a reconstitution of an extinct species of wild cattle, the aurochs. This experiment has proved interesting in opening up possibilities for us to see again creatures which are now extinct, but whose domestic descendants still carry some of the same genes in their bodies and cell structures. Even more important it brings home the fact that once extinguished a species is lost.

We still have wild animals basically unchanged by man even though he has made use of them for farming. The white park cattle and the Exmoor pony are two instances. The first of these are recognised now for their remarkable ability to withstand the effects of inbreeding. The

Dartmoor pony, close in type to the true wild horse

Exmoor pony is less widely recognised as valuable, but it is close in type to the true wild horse which roamed the cold wastes of central Europe during the last Ice Age. Its long, dense outer guard-hairs protect it from wind and rain and the soft underfur retains body heat, fitting the animal for a life in an unsympathetic environment. This, together with its ability to prosper in impoverished circumstances, marks the Exmoor and its less pure-bred cousin the Dartmoor as animals of supreme climatic adaptation.

The mealy muzzle colouring of the Exmoor and its light eye patches show a certain similarity to the horses depicted in the cave paintings of France and Spain. It has suffered from loss of its moorland habitat and the purity of the true semi-wild stock is threatened by cross-breeding, but this problem is well in hand and the future of the Exmoor is more secure than it has been for some time.

However, life in the countryside in late summer does not revolve around the animals; it looks forward to the harvest. The traditional fallow field system of farming, and the rotation of crops giving each field a period of rest, during which the fertility of the land was restored naturally by allowing weeds to grow such as wild clover and vetch and animals to graze, has disappeared in the past few years. The modern practice of using artificial fertilisers replaces the natural process to some degree, and two-crop rotation with cereals and other crops such as oil-seed rape is used.

Rape is the plant which makes June fields glow yellow with its flowers. It is a member of the cabbage family and produces seeds rich in oils and proteins. The problem is that the seeds are very small and require the use of an effectively sealed combine harvester so nothing is lost through gaps in the machine. However, to the wildlife of the field this practice is detrimental; no longer are dropped seeds there for the gleaning.

As August wanes and the harvest month of September appears on the horizon, a gleaner *par excellence* arrives in ever-growing numbers to harass picnickers and country dwellers alike. The wasps are at their peak numbers now and venture out to scour the surrounding countryside for sweet things. Although they do not store or even collect honey they have the same taste for sugary delicacies as their relatives the bees. Adult workers use sugar in the same way as humans, to provide necessary energy for daily tasks.

The grubs of the common wasp feed on caterpillars, spiders and insects which the adults paralyse with their stings before taking them to the larder in the depths of the colony, usually built underground in a mouse hole or even a disused rabbit hole. The nest, or comb, is not built from wax, but is made from a paper which they produce by shredding wood from fence posts or trees, mixing it with saliva to form a grey paste of very fine texture.

The wasp's larger, handsome and much-feared relative the hornet also builds a paper nest often in a hollow tree or barn, occasionally in the roof space of country cottages. A hornet sting can be exceedingly painful, but like the wasp it will rarely attack unless provoked. As hornets fly strong and high they do not usually mix up with people. Even so they can pose a real problem to the occupier if they do set up their colony in a house, and usually the only course of action is to resort to the good offices of the local pest officer, who will destroy them with poison.

By the end of August, providing there has been a settled spell of weather and the infamous August thunderstorms have kept their lowering faces below the sunlit horizon, the harvest will have begun. On the rolling downlands the combines thunder across the acres of waving gold grain leaving snail trails of straw behind them. Their flailing arms bid farewell to the cuckoo and the swift, who will soon leave us for the continent of Africa.

12

SEPTEMBER

September makes its sweeping entry and the scene is set with the brilliant colour of gold and the rich smell of a fruit cake, the promise of the autumn. The fruits of a million plants glitter in the hedgerows like so many jewels in a crown. In the morning the cool air greets the sun, a diadem of dewdrops sparkling from every spider's web.

Like man, the creatures of the countryside are preparing for the harvest. In the dry yellow forest of the cornfields mice skitter and scamper, but death stalks their every move as the stoat, that jaguar of the corn-stalks, glides through the rustling grain. Where the wind has flattened the crop and the ears lie close to the ground, woodpigeons and collared doves gorge themselves on the spilled seed, competing for food with the gaudy cock pheasants who soon will be forced by the beaters to show their flying prowess against the guns of the coming season.

In the streams the trout are now wary of the fly, so many of their number have been plucked from their natural element, but although the season is nearly over, with only the dog days remaining, a few stew-bred trout might still come eagerly. The hardened veterans of the stream lie beneath the fragmenting weedbeds sensing that the time of plenty will soon be gone.

Cock pheasant

Over the water one or two tardy swallows skim across the surface, picking up the final hatches of fly before joining the twittering martins on the telegraph wires. They are eager to be off, leaving an empty gap in our lives as the chill of autumn approaches.

The sights and sounds of the modern countryside are different from those of the past. The swing and swish of the bagging hook was replaced by the arm-waving rattle of the horse-drawn sail reaper and this in turn has been replaced by the combine harvester, a factory on wheels which cuts the grain, threshes the ripe seeds from the ears and spews out the chopped and useless stalks as it thunders across the landscape like a monster snail.

The new varieties of cereal are short in the straw so that modern machinery can deal with them more easily. There is little use nowadays for straw anyway. The older varieties of corn, barley and wheat stood tall on hollow golden stems – schoolchildren sucked their morning milk through these 'real' straws. These days straw is burned in the field, but it used to be a valuable commodity. Cottages were thatched with it, bricks were given bulk and binding power by adding straw, wattle and daub could not have existed without it and it kept animals warm and comfortable in barn, sty and stable.

Straw also meant stooks, which stood in the harvest field for about a week while the grain dried in the sun and wind. Then they were taken to the rickyard on horse-drawn waggons in the soft dusty evenings of late September and made into ricks prior to threshing.

All of these things belong to the past, and they were romantic only in retrospect; such harvests depended on cheap labour and lots of it, and desperately hard work it was too. The picturesque paintings and

222

photographs of families toiling in the fields do not show the torn muscles and grimed faces, the eyes red-rimmed with dust from the rickyard, the sheer exhaustion, that were the realities. Nevertheless our forefathers managed to wrest a good deal of enjoyment from the harvest, making a festival once the back-breaking work was done.

Threshing was a special time, with everyone getting together to give a hand, almost in holiday mood. In fact country children were usually given a school holiday timed to coincide with the harvest. They had to work hard as every pair of hands was needed, but it was fun and they looked forward to it with delightful anticipation, much as children today look forward to a trip to the seaside or a chance to see the cup final. They also knew they would be allowed to stay up late and listen to tales of harvests past.

Everything paled into insignificance and young and old were drawn to the farm rickyards at the threshing team's approach, entering the village rather like a circus. The box-operators, usually owner and son, were hired by the day. They travelled the countryside in a convoy, headed by a gleaming brass-bound traction engine, belching steam and smoke and pulling the brightly painted wooden box thresher with carving all around its frame, picked out in different colours. The wheels and drive pulleys were usually painted red and the peripheries were polished by the flying leather and canvas drive-belts. Behind the thresher, bringing up the rear of the convoy, was a kind of caravan, a wheeled contraption not unlike a shepherd's hut but with tongue-and-groove boarded walls and tiny windows with bright curtains and a curved corrugated iron roof. This was home for the threshing contractor and his companion whilst they were on the road.

Inside it contained all the necessary comforts in miniature. Between the folding bunks, which let down from the boarded walls, was an iron pot-bellied stove providing warmth and a means of cooking. Box chests built into the walls for storage doubled as seats. This waggon ran on solid iron-tyred wheels and in the hilly Devon terrain two necessary pieces of equipment were the brakes and slowing shoes. These were iron wedges placed between the wheels and the road with a curved groove in the wedge-shaped upper surface into which the rim of the wheel was run so that it could not turn.

On the steepest hills slowing shoes would be used as well as brakes, and the whole assemblage would rumble down striking sparks from the road surface as the skids wedged the wheels and the brakes smoked under the friction.

The actual threshing machine was connected to the engine via a series of uncovered driving belts which flashed and waved like ribbons as the assemblage was set in motion in the rickyard. The workers gathered to start the most vital of harvest functions, the separation of grain from ear and the collection of the cleaned grain into bags for storage and sale. The work of forking the stooks of corn into the gaping dust-spewing maw of the threshing machine was hard and tiring and as the rick was consumed the work grew even harder: without an elevator the stooks had to be forked up to the man on the top of the machine. As the rick became smaller the excitement of the village boys mounted, for they knew that the rats and mice who had found shelter there would be driven out into the open.

The rickyard was surrounded by wire netting so no rats could escape and the boys, armed with sticks, eagerly awaited the last level when the rats would scurry, squeaking, from their shelter. Pandemonium reigned as the dogs, who had been sitting quietly in wet-tongued anticipation, caught sight of their quarry. Sticks flew and dogs barked and yelped excitedly, men and boys yelled and the rats screeched.

Then as quickly as it started the whole thing was over and the men sat and smoked black twist in short pipes and talked of the yield, discussing the merits of this harvest against others, telling tales of rats as big as cats and how old Cecil's ferret had been found in the base of the rick. Their job done, the circus of the threshers left the village, the bright machines dustier than when they had made their triumphal entry several days before. The village returned to normal.

The old traction engine was quite unlike its modern diesel-powered counterpart which is purely functional. It was more like the heavy horse in character, for it needed to be tended and cared for, fed with coal, watered regularly and groomed till the brasses of the spinning governor shone like gold in the autumn sunshine. Most of them were built in the early half of the twentieth century by companies who took pride in the quality of their workmanship and the lasting value of their engineering. Consequently quite a few still survive, as attendances at modern steam-engine rallies show. They are as popular now as ever they were.

The magic of traction engines comes not so much from their power, which is enormous, but from their personality, the way they obey the driver and the quality they possess of seeming to breathe as they work; the harder the task, the deeper they inhale the steam from their boilers, and the more smoke they exhale from their brass-bound chimney stacks. Even the steering has certain similarities with a horse's harness,

Traction engine – the iron horse

the front axle being pulled around on its pivot point by chains to links which look like bit-swivels; control over direction is achieved by a tiny wheel which the driver rotates frantically to negotiate even the gentlest bend in the road.

Their progress through the autumn countryside was slow and majestic, akin to an elephant's progress through the jungle. Unhurried and oblivious of obstacles they trundled along the country roads, the canopy above the whirling flywheel and polished brass dials and valves resembling a howdah on a Maharajah's favourite beast.

Old West Country apple trees, bent like old men with arthritis, are covered with a grey and hoary lichen, which gave each village its own particular smell of woodsmoke. Lichen will only thrive where the air is pure and when fires burned in the autumn the smell was like incense on the evening breeze. Open fires were not burned just to warm cold bodies. They were the chief means of cooking, and the inglenook fireplace was supremely functional, with racks like black iron saws whereon hung the pots and the ever-boiling huge iron kettles encrusted with soot. It also provided a home for that peculiar and homely fireside creature the hearth cricket. How many hours must have been spent searching for these elusive ventriloquists without success. After locating the source of the trill, closer inspection causes the creature to stop its song and the hunt ends in frustration. One of its relatives who has suffered from modernisation in the countryside is the field cricket. It can now be heard, filling the night air with its chirrups, only in more remote and agriculturally less advanced parts of the country.

Another sad casualty is the glow-worm, the lantern-keeper of the ditch, whose pale greenish light, shining from even the darkest part of the hedgerow, was such a feature of country lanes a mere twenty years ago. Insecticides have reduced its numbers, but the major cause of its decline is the removal of hedges and the fact that the males were lured away from the dimly-lit females to brighter – but sterile! – street lights.

This fascinating little creature, whose light is produced by the action of bacteria in the female's body, is a member of the firefly family, a northern representative of the bright flashing species of tropical or semi-tropical beetles. It used to be the main predator of snails in many parts of rural England, but these also have declined and it is highly likely that this impedes their recolonisation of areas where formerly they were common.

In the woodlands there is a new splash of colour on the forest floor, and in the hedges too. The bright red caps of fungi are expanding to take advantage of the damp warm soil to flower, filling the gentle breezes with millions of tiny spores. Fungi and bacteria are the fulcrum on which the fertility of the natural countryside pivots. These plants, whose fruiting bodies appear above ground at this time of year, break down the vegetable matter into a form which can be used by other higher chlorophyll-bearing organisms. Without fungi, meadowland would become choked with dead plant matter.

The most familiar in this group of plants in the British Isles is the mushroom, a succulent addition to many a favourite dish. In the misty September mornings the white mushrooms can be seen dotting the cobweb-garlanded grass in a favoured meadow, especially where horses have been allowed to graze and where the ground is fertile, rich and warm. A diligent searcher who has risen early can often gather pounds of the tasty white caps.

Mushrooms are not the only culinary delicacies. Wood blewitts come into this category and so does the rare and pungent truffle which can be found in English beech woods. However, fungi are not a group to experiment or take liberties with. The chances of finding a variety which can cause violent stomach pains at the least and death at the worst are quite high and a few wild fungi contain hallucinatory drugs. The old tales of people being possessed by demons are thought to have originated from cases of hallucinations caused by fungus poisoning.

The most infamous cause of hallucinations is ergot, the rust fungus of cereal crops which has caused outbreaks of serious illness in the past. Anyone eating bread made from contaminated grain absorbed the poison into their system. The substance ergotamine, derived from this fungus, has been used in medicines, and life-saving drugs such as penicillin are made from moulds, the same basic group of organisms as fungi. The healing power of antibiotics was known long before Sir Alexander Fleming discovered the mould growing in a dish on a windowsill at Paddington Hospital where he worked. Country folk had long used cheese mould to cure cuts and skin infections on animals. And, of course, yeast has been used for centuries to prepare staple foods and drinks; without it there would be no bread as we know it today and no cider either.

Cider making has been the province of south-country people for thousands of years. It was probably brought there from the Normandy area of France long ago when tin was traded with other items from the continent where cider is even older than West Country scrumpy. Cider was not originally made by accident, unlike mead, although the two have been brought together as a blend and very fine it is too. The preparation of a fermented drink from apple juice requires certain conditions of climate and temperature before the raw fruit can be converted into the heady Devon and Somerset brews. The apples which produce cider are special too and have been evolved over the years for their particular combination of acid and sugar which gives the drink its alcohol content and special flavour.

Most West Country villages possessed their own cider press, although by the early 1940s many had largely fallen into disuse. The press consisted of a massive oak beam supported and secured by oak uprights. The beam was designed to accept a screw thread and a lever which lowered the pressure plate down on to a tray also made of oak. At cider-pressing time this tray was lined with hessian sacks and straw, and the chopped fruit placed in it. This was topped with straw and a further layer of pulp, the process being carried on until the press was full. The stack of pulp and straw was known as the 'cheese'. Then the pressure plate was lowered by the screw until the juice flowed from a hole in the tray into barrels, where it was allowed to ferment under the influence of wild yeasts present on the fruit. The ferment was short and violent if the weather was warm, long and quiet if it was cold, and the variation in the speed of ferment and in the sugar content of the apples meant that the drink was inconsistent and bitter. It also tended to be straw-coloured and cloudy. Nevertheless it was drunk with relish and pronounced the finest available, which was not strictly true because usually the local brewery produced a far more acceptable rough cider which the villagers consumed by the gallon at their local inn.

Modern scrumpy is a far more palatable drink, with little resemblance to the cloudy brew of old. The throng of visitors who down quantities of scrumpy would probably not have given a second look to 'real' scrumpy, which it was said would turn your liver to stone.

Other fruits ripening to fullness now include the bright red glossy bryony berries, on stems which twist and turn around the hawthorn; the hawthorn berries themselves, hard as stone, wait for the first frost and the winter's fieldfares and redwings to arrive. Horse chestnuts smile like french-polished globes as they spill from their spiny seed cases when they hit the earth, to the joy of all small boys. Beech mast patters its triangles of buttery seeds on the woodland floor where mice and squirrels gorge themselves to fatness for the approaching winter.

Beech mast or beech nuts are an unreliable crop. Some years, when conditions have been good in the preceeding spring, the trees produce such a vast quantity of the shiny triangular fruit that the ground

Nuts nibbled by dormouse

228

beneath is massed with fallen shells. Yet in other years the inconspicuous flowers have been killed, by frost or drought, and the tree will produce nothing. Such an event drastically affects the natural economy of the beechwood. It puts small mammals and seed-eating birds on a starvation diet for the winter, causing them to move outside the wood for food, becoming prey to all the attendant dangers. Thankfully it is rare for all wild fruit and nut crops to fail in one year and the consistent oak can be relied upon to produce protein enough to tide hungry mice and squirrels and other animals over the lean months.

Edible dormouse

Everywhere the wild creatures are beginning to stock up their larders. Dormice are fattening on the ripe fruit and hedgehogs start the process of laying down a store of fat under their skin. Even the insects are responding as the year's clock winds down. Wasps blunder over the blackberries gorging on the ripe fruit. Their toil is almost over and the tiredness of autumn is with them. Soon they will die, worn out with all the frantic activity of the preceeding months. The honeybees are busy collecting nectar from the remaining flowers, such as buddleia and the misty sedum, which thoughtful gardeners grow particularly to encourage the butterflies who jostle wing-to-wing with fat indolent bumble bees, competing for the sugary liquid.

Buddleias attract a great many butterflies. Peacocks vie with red admirals, pushing the small tortoiseshells away from the banquet. When the wind and weather permits foreigners come too, painted ladies from across the Channel. Usually they are limited to a few special areas, but there are times when there is a mass immigration: then they can be seen flying like clouds of confetti across the southern coast.

Clouded yellow on clover

Another butterfly which is an occasional visitor, but can appear in vast numbers during favourable years, is the clouded yellow, a beautiful insect with pale orange wings and a fast buoyant flight. It will lay eggs in this country on its food plant, clover, but more usually it is simply a brief flash of colour soon gone, leaving only a memory.

Our native butterflies are nearly all over now. Only the large garden butterflies are seen in anything like their summer profusion, but among the blackthorn a rare late hatcher, the brown hairstreak, skips from bush to bush seeking the twigs on which the female will lay her eggs before joining the debris of the summer in the hedge-bottom. Goldfinches flutter around the oil-rich thistle seedheads, their yellow barred wings throwing up clouds of thistledown which collects in drifts in the hedge-bottom. As the leaves turn to gold matching the goldfinch's wing, the robin in the hazel thicket changes his song to the sad winter refrain that he will chant until spring.

Out in the open fields the harvest is in full swing, and the September air reverberates far into the evening with the sound of the combine and the grain being taken to the silo and the barn. The straw lies in lines in the quiet fields and pheasants come out of the woods to glean the dropped seed.

Times have changed, but the bygones remaining in museums and private collections give us an insight into the lives of our forefathers. Apart from the dangers from disease, and the larger work load borne by each member of the community before machines took over heavy tasks, the life of the farmers was not so very different from what it is now. They were always dependent upon the weather and for generations before the tractor they had a few machines, masterpieces of human ingenuity: fan winnowers to separate the grain from the chaff, sophisticated ploughs which needed only the power of horses to drive them through the soil, the brilliant, exquisite waterwheel to mastermind the grinding of corn.

For industry too, all over the land, streams and rivers were harnessed to provide power to operate heavy hammers and drive the mechanism of textile-processing machines in the eighteenth century. The history of many mills echoes the history of the communities they served. A lot of mills are still capable of performing the task for which they were originally designed. Some have existed for nearly 1,000 years and the stream which fills the leat may have powered more than one mill on its watercourse.

Watermills project a sense of peace and power combined which is hard to find in modern machinery. Although they possess immense horsepower there is no feeling of menace. The mill wheel, like the plough horse, must be cared for to give of its best. If left untended a horse will wander; a mill wheel will overheat and spoil the dressing of the wheel, or at worst set fire to the mill building.

The windmill is another engine of the elements. It has the look of a dancer, seemingly fragile, but actually sturdily built to catch the most ephemeral of the elements, the breeze. Not for it the howling gale; it needs a steady gentle blow to propel the whirling sails.

The first windmills were 'post mills', some of which still remain and have been lovingly restored to their former glory. In this type of mill the whole structure faced the wind and was balanced on a massive central pillar made mostly of oak. It was not until several centuries later that the post mill was grafted onto the top of a solid wooden structure to take advantage of the wind blowing above tree-top level. In Victorian times the countryside was dotted with the waving revolving sails of windmills, evolved from the relatively primitive structure of the post mill, which had to be turned into the wind by means of a beam pushed around by hand or by horse. Later versions faced the prevailing breeze steered by means of a weather-vane sail.

Gradually the mills fell into disuse and were converted into dwellings or just left to fall to pieces and be demolished. There has been a revival of windmill power over the last two decades, but it will be a long time before it is widely used again, if indeed this ever happens in our power-hungry society. It is still used in the fens to pump water from drainage ditches, but the windmill is expensive to run and maintain, erratic in the performance it can offer, and is disappearing rapidly.

Autumn is beginning to make itself felt in the ponds and streams now and creatures grown fat in the days of plenty are preparing for the lean times ahead. Frogs return to the muddy fastness in preparation for the winter sleep and caddis-fly larvae build their homes of sticks and twigs cemented together with glue exuded from their bodies. Then they make their way across the ooze to deeper water. The shorter days are beginning to be reflected in reduced plant growth, including the algae on which minute creatures such as daphnia depend. The hopping

Rainbow trout

hordes of the water margins which provide food for a variety of insects and fish are declining in numbers, but the lowering water temperatures make the trout more active as the oxygen level increases.

In the Scottish rivers salmon are running up from the sea in the long-awaited autumn run. In recent years these runs have been reduced due to the effect of netting at sea and the disease ulcerated dermal necrosis (UDN) which has decimated fish stocks in many of our more important salmon rivers. Fortunately there has been a decline in the incidence of this disease in the last year or two, so perhaps the dreamed-of run up the river Thames will not be affected.

Salmon need pure, highly oxygenated water and the finest indicators of purity are two of the less glamorous occupants of a river, the minnow and the crayfish; both creatures have a very low tolerance to impurities. The crayfish is mainly found in chalk streams, for it needs the dissolved natural salts to build its armoured shell. The acid water of peat-fed streams is not at all to its liking. These small freshwater members of the lobster family are vital in many river systems, fulfilling a scavenging function in the deep pools and quiet eddies vital to the purity of the water.

They can be eaten and are quite tasty, but as they are only about 5 in long they do not make much of a mouthful and catching them for food is no longer generally popular, merely an enjoyable hobby. They are mainly nocturnal and do their job of keeping the river clean during the hours of darkness. A powerful lamp shone into the water near a fast-flowing stretch, or under the sill of a weir, will show if they are present, but they are not visible for long and dart away very quickly by propelling themselves through the water backwards, like their marine cousins, by strong flicks of their broad tails. In the Chiltern chalk streams, where pollution of the glass-clear water is mercifully low, crayfish are quite common. They used to form a special part of the otter's diet when otters too were common.

They are preparing for the winter now and by this time their young, which the female carries in a pouch beneath her body, are free swimming and independent. The green and brown adults build up reserves of food to tide them over the lean times. They are very like their seagoing relatives to look at, armed with two strong pincers with which they will defend themselves against prying fingers.

Water is the basis of any countryside and pure uncontaminated springs, streams and rivers are vital for the survival of many wild creatures. Organisations like the Thames Water Authority have realised this and have taken steps to ensure the quality of the water in one of the most highly populated areas in Great Britain. This attitude has made south-east England the envy of Europe and given an example to others of what can be done.

The year in the countryside is drawing to its close and in villages and towns people are enjoying the harvest supper. Churches all across the land hold thanksgiving services for the harvest and the fruits of the fields, altars piled high with traditional loaves baked in the shape of a wheatsheaf and sheaves of real cereals, bringing home to all of us our dependence on the land and all growing things.

It was thought that an accidental chance hybridisation of two types of grass produced the first cereal grain in the Middle East. Another chance meeting of that grain and our remote ancestors who invented the plough led, through the ages, to the modern technological era of machines that we enjoy today, giving us immense power and the ability to change the natural world for good or ill.

We have a responsibility to use our knowledge to the greater benefit of the world, natural and unnatural, in which we live. The natural world could manage quite well without our presence, but we cannot manage without the plant kingdom to convert the sun's radiant energy into energy which we can use. Even the fossil fuels on which our modern life style depends so heavily were once green plants growing in the light of that same sun 1,000 million years ago.

The few men who have left the security of earth and viewed it from the firmament have all experienced a sense of wonder at its beauty and colour. It spins like a living sapphire set against the soft velvet of infinity. It may not be unique in the countless galaxies existing in the incomprehensible vastness of space, but to us, the custodians of the planet earth, it is the only world we have and we must treasure it for the jewel it is; to pass on as a legacy to generations as yet unborn.

ACKNOWLEDGEMENTS

I would like to thank the following people for their help during the production of this book:

The Editor and staff of the Hertfordshire and Bedfordshire *Evening Post-Echo*; the photographers of the *Post-Echo* who guided me in the technique of photography, especially Peter Hoare who took my photograph for the jacket and John Jones for his photograph of frogs and frogspawn on page 87; Richard Revels for supplying the excellent photographs on pages 12, 72, 80, 131, 132, 210; Alan Southgate for his assistance with photographic processing; and Bernard Double for allowing me to use old photographs of his family and providing me with his family history.

Also Gordon Beningfield for his companionship in our wanderings through Wessex; John and Barbara Wilson for their help and advice; David Curry of Plymouth City Museum for his technical advice on obscure points of natural history and palaeontology; and the Finch Foundry Trust and Sticklepath Museum of Rural Industry, Okehampton, Devon.

Last, but not least, my thanks to Ann, my wife, whose tireless efforts in typing and proof-reading etc, made the whole process of writing this book infinitely more enjoyable.

INDEX

Numbers in *italic* type denote line drawings; numbers in **bold** denote photographs.

237